Seasons
of a
Woman's
Life

Seasons of a Woman's Life

Lois Evans

MOODY PRESS
CHICAGO

André Crouch. "Throught It All." Copyright 1971. Renewed by MANNA MUSIC, INC., 35255 Brooten Road, Pacific City, OR 97135. All Rights Reserved. Used by Permission.

All Scripture quotations, unless otherwise indicated, are taken from the *New King James Version*. Copyright © 1982 by Thomas Nelson, Inc. Used by permission. All rights reserved.

Scripture quotations marked NIV are taken from the *Holy Bible, New International Version®*. NIV®. Copyright © 1973, 1978, 1984 by International Bible Society. Used by permission of Zondervan Publishing House. All rights reserved.

Library of Congress Cataloging-in-Publication Data

Evans, Lois, 1949–
    Seasons of a woman's life / by Lois Evans.
        p. cm.
    ISBN 0-8024-8592-8
    1. Christian women--Religious life. 2. Christian life--Biblical teaching. I. Title.

BV4527 .E897 2000
248.8´43--dc21

00-057884

3 5 7 9 10 8 6 4 2

Printed in the United States of America

*Never be afraid to trust an unknown future to
an all-knowing God.
He who believes in God
Is not careful for the morrow,
But labors joyfully and with a great heart.
He must work and watch
Yet never be anxious or careful,
But commit all to Him,
And live in serene tranquility
With a quiet heart, as one who sleeps
Safely and quietly.*

—MARTIN LUTHER

For who knows whether
God has called you to the Kingdom
for such a time as this?

Dedicated to

My parents, James Basil and Annie Eleen Cannings,
for investing your time, dedication, love, and longsuffering
in bringing me face-to-face with my Savior.
Then modelling before me a confidence in an all-knowing God.
Thanks, Daddy and Mummy.

Also my husband, Tony,
who always encourages me to grow and develop.
He takes the time to listen, challenge,
and patiently advise in my continued growth.
Thanks for giving me an opportunity and
for being there for me
as we continue to grow through the seasons together.
I know as long as God gives me life, you will be my cheerleader.

Thanks to my faithful sister, Elizabeth,
for being there for me and our four children and grandchild,
who have given me the joys of motherhood many times over.

Thanks also to Mrs. Ann Vanberg,
whose encouraging words, "This is only for a season,"
redirected and realigned the focus of my life's journey.

Contents

Foreword

I have had the awesome privilege and joy of being married to Lois Evans for over thirty years. As her husband, I have watched her move through the seasons of a woman's life. I have seen her endure with strength the trials of winter. I have seen her grow and flourish in the beauty of springtime. I have seen her struggle in the heat of summer, and I have seen her change with the cool of fall.

It is because I have personally observed Lois address the seasons in her own life that I know every woman will be blessed who reads this book. You see, Lois is not writing about what she has heard or read but what she has personally experienced. It is because she has tried changing her experiences to the changelessness of God's Word that she has been able to live such a consistent, stable, and victorious Christian life.

What Lois shares in this book will be a blessing to every woman who reads it because the principles, thoughts, and challenges she shares come from a genuine heart and a very real person. Raising a family, supporting a workaholic husband, helping to develop a local church, and managing a national ministry gives Lois the credentials to share what she shares in this work.

It is because I know that what you are about to read is laced with the blood, sweat, and tears of real life that I know it will not only inform you, but encourage your heart. Many people know Tony Evans the preacher; far fewer know Lois Evans the singer and speaker. Many know Tony Evans the leader; fewer know Lois Evans the inspirer. Many know Tony Evans the ministry builder; fewer know Lois Evans the ministry organizer. Many know Tony Evans the visionary; few know Lois Evans the prayer warrior. Many know Tony Evans the family man; fewer know Lois Evans the homemaker. It's time I move to the shadows so you can get to know the real reason why so many know me. It's because God gave me a woman who knows Him and who has experienced Him as she has moved through her seasons of life. It's the same God who will walk with you as you move through your season of life.

TONY EVANS

Introduction

All around America and all around the world, God has blessed me with wonderful opportunities to speak to women—women of all ages, races, and social status. After I speak, when I'm able to talk to these women one-on-one, I am privileged to hear about their wishes, their wants, and their worries. I hear their longings for blessing—blessings for their families as well as for themselves. I hear the cry of their hearts because of unexpected disappointments, heartaches, and frustrations. And wherever I talk to women, I hear the same question asked in many different ways. Whatever their age, whatever their responsibilities, women want to know,

Will it always be like this?

The answer to that question is almost always "No." And the reason I can safely say, "No, life will not always be like it is today," is because of a very important principle. Sometimes we hear the saying "All things must pass." That is true, at least in earthly terms. But there's a more specific principle at work than that. The Lord has shown me that women are seasonal creatures, and when we look at our lives in light of the season we are in, we are better able to cope with some of the challenges and are more likely to appreciate the blessings—while we still have them.

For example, it may seem that we'll never reach the end of changing diapers, driving car pools, or dealing with teenage upheaval. Then all at once we find ourselves in a new situation. The children have grown up a little or a lot; they've gone off to kindergarten or off to college. Suddenly we have time on our hands. We have less to do; we have different things to face. God has brought us into another time of life during which we will have new discoveries to make, new roles to play, and new blessings to enjoy.

In short, the season has changed.

I've found out a great deal about seasons in my own personal life. I was born in Guyana, South America, into a Christian home, and although I did not receive Him personally until the age of twelve, from an early age I heard the good news of Jesus Christ. I have godly parents who raised us in the Word and in church. My mother prayed for all of her children, that each of us would come to know the Lord and serve Him.

I remember how hard it was for Mom to raise us. Dad's job took him all over the country, so Mom was often alone at home with eight kids. I remember the times when she was tired of all the hard work and the lack of material things. Despite the hardships, she faithfully honored her season of life, and I often heard her say, "For the Lord's name's sake . . . I am going to keep my commitment to Him and to you kids."

Even now, when things become overwhelming for me and I hear myself asking the age-old question, "What for?" I hear that familiar voice answer, "For the Lord's name's sake."

Even with such a large family, our mom still found time every day to have devotions with us, and the Scriptures that I remember most clearly today are the ones I learned at her knee and in Sunday school. Dearest to my heart is my Life Verse, found in John 15:5. "I am the vine, you are the branches. He who abides in me, and I in him, bears much fruit; for without Me you can do nothing."

I know Scripture is true; I believe it with my whole heart. In fact, the meaning of that verse is buried so deeply in my heart that I never tackle anything unless I get clear direction from Him. Why? Because only then can I be sure that He will see me through.

I'll tell you more about my own experiences later in the book. But besides learning about life's seasons from my own walk with God, I've also learned many lessons from the biblical story of Esther. God had an important plan for Esther's life, and He led her through a specific process of preparation until she was ready to fulfill His will. Only after He had prepared her properly was she able to say yes to His will and to see that she had come into the kingdom *for such a time as this.*

What do I mean by seasons? We often think of the word in terms of spring, summer, winter, and fall. But I like to think of our life seasons as seed-planting, growth, and harvest.

During the *Season of Seed-Planting,* the Lord calls us to Himself. We commit ourselves to His service, and we enjoy communion with Him. This often takes place while we are still single, before we meet the man God has chosen for us. While we are single, we can devote ourselves to building our personal relationship with God through Jesus Christ, cherishing Him as our First Love.

The King's court is made up of single and married women. God chooses women in each state and leads them into the *Season of Growth,* which encompasses lessons in obedience, service, and preparation. Just as Esther was taught to be a proper wife to a great king, we also grow up in the King's court being tutored in self-discipline, sacrifice, and serenity. That is God's way of preparing us for our particular future in Him.

At last we enter the *Season of Harvest.* We are finally ready to step into the primary responsibilities for which we have been prepared. During this season, we learn to be content without becoming complacent; we learn to say yes to God's direction, even when it means stepping out of our comfort zone. And we learn the blessings of fulfillment as we see God's plan for our lives being brought to pass.

What is God's purpose for your life? Have you discovered it yet? Just as Esther found herself in the unique position of saving her people from certain death, I am grateful to say that God has made it possible for me to reach out to others whose lives are at risk spiritually, emotionally, or even physically. But without His guidance, without abiding in Him, without learning the lessons implicit in each season of my life, I would be of little use to Him today. Apart from Him, I can do nothing.

It is essential for God's women to learn about their seasons because He has a unique plan for each of us. In Psalm 139 we read that God ordered our days before we were ever born. And submitting to His unique path for us will help us keep our balance as we navigate through the many choices that make themselves available to us throughout the years.

Today's Christian women are being pressed on every side to conform to standards of this world. Unique opportunities in the areas of education and business have opened doors to women that were not available even half a century ago. While on the one hand Christian women should enjoy the benefits of these opportunities, we must be careful not to let this world system rearrange our biblical priorities.

Our first priority as women is to maintain a vital personal relationship with God. Proverbs 31:30 says, "Charm is deceitful and beauty is vain, but a woman who fears the Lord, she shall be praised." This "fear" is awe-filled respect that flows out of an ongoing relationship with God. Our jobs, careers, and degrees must never overrule our daily intimacy and interaction with our Savior. An ongoing awareness of His Presence and a devotion to His Word will give us stability, confidence, and direction as we pursue the various ministries God calls us into during each season of our lives.

The second priority for us as Christian women in this quickly changing society is our commitment to our families. The family is too easily being written off the world's agenda. Nonetheless, our status in society must never overshadow our responsibility to our status at home. Titus 2:5 clearly states that women should "be discreet, chaste, homemakers, good, obedient to their own husbands, that the word of God may not be blasphemed."

This does not mean that women have to stay home (the virtuous women of Proverbs 31 had a job). Rather, it is saying that above all else we should make sure that the home is being properly taken care of. How many times have we seen a woman with a great career who has not provided a strong, loving home for her children? That kind of ungodly prioritizing always ends up in a great mess for all concerned.

Finally, we Christian women should seek to be the best we can be no matter into what field of service God has called us. We should use our privileged position in society to further the cause of Christ in the world. Esther is a good example of this. God gave her an unparalleled position as queen of a mighty nation, and she chose to use it to bring deliverance to the Jews. Have you ever asked yourself how you could use your position in society as an opportunity to further the cause of Christ?

By being the best for God that you possibly can be in the midst of your responsibilities, you will "let your light so shine before men, that they may see your good works and glorify your Father in heaven" (Matthew 5:16). In this quickly changing world, God needs strong, stable Christian women who demonstrate a divine orientation to life. Can you think of a more wonderful, more rewarding calling?

In the pages that follow, we'll consider Esther's life and I'll share with you my own experiences and those of other women. I think you'll find helpful principles, familiar feelings, and encouraging promises as you read. Together, we'll consider the kind of seeds He is planting in our hearts, the type of growth He anticipates, and the abundant harvest He expects from us as He leads us through the seasons of a woman's life. For He has said,

> *I know the thoughts that I think toward you, . . .*
> *thoughts of peace and not of evil,*
> *to give you a future and a hope.*
> —JEREMIAH 29:11

PART
ONE

The
Season
of
Seed-
Planting

CHAPTER ONE

The Call

*Now in Shushan the citadel there was a certain Jew
whose name was Mordecai. . . .
And Mordecai had brought up Hadassah, that is, Esther,
his uncle's daughter, for she had neither father nor mother.
The young woman was lovely and beautiful.
When her father and mother died,
Mordecai took her as his own daughter.*

—ESTHER 2:5,7

The first seed that should be planted in the heart of a godly woman is the seed of God's call. But what does it mean to be called by God? Every woman who walks with the Lord has a different story to tell about how He reached out and drew her to Himself. My own story centers on the influence of my family.

If you read the story of Esther, you'll see that she came from the culture of the Jews. They were believers in the Lord with a rich tradition of faith and godliness. Like Esther, tradition and spiritual mentors also surrounded me. My parents and family lived a devout life in front of me, so it was easy and natural for me to believe and accept the importance of God's call.

At the age of twelve, when I said yes to Jesus Christ, I made a decision to be His disciple. I knew that meant that I would be different. I knew I would be required to have a testimony for Him. I knew that He wanted me to make a difference in the world. And where did I receive that type of information? Again, I received it from my traditions—from the words and actions of my parents.

LISTENING FOR YOUR CALL

Why does God call us, planting the seed of discipleship in our hearts? He calls us because He loves us. He calls us because, before the foundation of the world, each of us was foreseen and designed in every intricate detail. If you haven't read Psalm 139, this would be a good time for you to do so. You'll discover there that God had your days ordered before you were ever born.

Once you answer His loving call, at the point of salvation, you enter into that glorious, divine plan, devised especially for you by our Sovereign God. Salvation calls you into a new relationship with God for all eternity. You are not a chance happening. You are one of a kind. There is no one else on this planet that has your plan. That's why you can relax in the face of trouble and temptation, because you are more than a conqueror in Jesus Christ.

There are many wonderful Scriptures that speak of our salvation. In Romans 5 we read that even though we were doomed for a lost eternity, God reached down and saved us. "Therefore, just as through one man sin entered the world, and death through sin, and thus death spread to all men, because all sinned" (Romans 5:12).

Despite our sin, He made a way out of no way.

"If you confess with your mouth the Lord Jesus and believe in your heart that God has raised Him from the dead, you will be saved. For with the heart one believes to righteousness, and with the mouth confession is made to salvation" (Romans 10:9–10).

Some people will not make it into God's heaven, even though their pardon has already been signed. Jesus has signed it, but we have to personally receive it. That means answering His call. And once you have received Him, you are transformed into a new creation. Do you realize how exciting that is to have another chance, and this time to do everything with the help and encouragement of the Holy Spirit?

Maybe you have forgotten who you really are. If so, please let me remind you. If you have received Jesus Christ into your life, you are a joint heir with Him. That means everything that happened to Jesus is afforded to us as believers. He died, and we too have to die daily to the things of this world. He Himself told us that we would suffer persecution. But that's not the end of the story. He arose, and we arise with Him in victory and power. If we live life focusing on who we are—joint heirs with Christ—we can get through the difficult times, because there is hope. There is joy ahead. There is a promise waiting to be fulfilled.

Just as God has chosen each of us for a particular plan and purpose, God also chose people in the Old Testament. They sometimes found themselves in trouble due to their disobedience. In the book of Esther, the Jews were in bondage, having been taken captive by the mighty Persian kingdom. But Mordecai, Esther's uncle and guardian, was a godly man who continued to wail and bemoan before God his people's desperate need. He knew he could call on God because God had called on him and the rest of the Jews to be His people.

When desperate needs come up in our lives, we tend to forget who we are and to whom we belong. If we have responded to His call, the Lord can take care of our problems. He can even use the bad and the ugly issues of our past and begin weaving them together into His kingdom plan.

God had a significant purpose for Esther in history. She lived every day knowing that she was His child and that something good was going to come out of the Jews' difficult circumstances. She placed her confidence in God and trusted the wisdom of her uncle Mordecai. We, too, should place all our confidence in an all-knowing God. And we should spend time listening to those who know God really well, those who will go to God on our behalf.

Our Higher Calling

Many women are satisfied to be saved and on their way to heaven, not realizing that the Lord has a divine purpose for them on earth. Each woman the Lord calls to Himself is designed to use her gifts, talents, and skills to promote His kingdom. God does more than call us into salvation. He calls us into His service. Salvation offers to each of us a new purpose in history.

But maybe you're asking yourself an important question: *What exactly is God's call? Is it a voice in the night? Is it a sign in the heavens? How can we recognize God's call?*

I believe that God's call is a compulsion you just can't shake. No matter how hard you try, it keeps coming up. Is there something like that in your life? Is there something you keep avoiding? Why don't you talk it over with your Christian friends and ask God for confirmation of it? Then, once you're sure it's His call, say, "Yes, Lord!" You needn't worry. Whatever His call requires of you, He will provide you with the resources to get the job done. What's more, you will experience the matchless joy of knowing that you are right where you belong.

Besides that unrelenting call, God also orchestrates people, places, and things in our lives in order to lead us to the place He has for us. As we focus on Him, He steers us into His perfect will (Proverbs 3:5–6). God orchestrated events for Esther so that she was in the right place at the right time. Then Mordecai's wise guidance helped her look beyond herself to something much bigger. In my own life, God used godly parents to bring me into His plan for me. Every aspect of my call, from personal salvation to practical service, was uniquely orchestrated by God.

Salvation gives us resurrection power. Salvation brings us into God's adopted family. Salvation also delivers us from a purposeless existence. Esther could go on, overcoming her fears and following her instructions, because she had a goal in mind. By God's grace, individuals who held the same principles surrounded her.

Our call is an invitation into a uniquely designed life role, a role that God has equipped us to carry out. When Esther ascended to the Persian throne, it was more than a Cinderella story come true. God had moved her into a strategic position for His purposes. Not only had Esther's physical and temperamental loveliness propelled her far beyond the competition, but she also went on to show that she was mentally tough enough to handle a position of responsibility.

THE SMART BLACK BOOK

In order to effectively respond to our calling, it is essential that we walk with God on a daily basis and that we build ourselves up in His Word. This will prepare us for the unknown, unpredictable, and unexpected events that will surely come along in our service to Him. Every one of us who is called by God to serve is also called to "be diligent to present [himself] approved to God, a worker who does not need to be ashamed, rightly dividing the word of truth" (2 Timothy 2:15).

One of the women on staff at our ministry, The Urban Alternative, was once in the army. She told me about some of the strange tasks she was given to do during military training. "Sometimes," she explained, "we were told to take boxes from one side of the room to the other and then back again. We were supposed to place the boxes back where we got them from, and then repeat this same process. When we asked the sergeant why, he would yell, 'Just do what I say!'"

The purpose of this exercise was, of course, to see if the recruits could follow orders, even when the orders didn't seem to make much sense. Sometimes the things that happen in our lives don't seem to make sense, either. That's why it is so important for us to store up the Word in our hearts and to build strong confidence in an all-knowing God. That way, we will obey Him without doubts and questions because we will have learned to trust Him implicitly.

This same woman went on to tell me about the "Smart Black Book." The army provides this book of instructions to be kept within reach by all personnel. Even when the soldiers were asleep, the book was always next to their beds because they had to be able to find instructions and information in case of an emergency. If the soldiers did not have the smart book with them, they were punished by having to do a large number of push-ups.

God's Word is much like that black book. Everything we need to know about life is inside. Do you have the smart book with you always, both in your hand and in your heart? Or will you have to do a lot of spiritual push-ups because you have been negligent? We need God's Word to continually remind us that the One who can save us can also keep us. And He has promised to bring to fulfillment the desires of our heart.

Now, that doesn't mean we always *feel* like our desires are being fulfilled. One of the challenges we face as we pass through the seasons of our life is our own impatience. We are always yearning to move on, to get to the next season, to arrive at some future goal, to settle down into some kind of joyous fulfillment. When we are single, we long to be married. When we have little children, we long for them to grow up. When we are working in a career position, we long to stay home and care for the home and family. When we are homemakers, we long to be moneymakers.

There are four seasons in the year: spring, summer, fall, and winter. Now, you can sit in on a particularly hot day and complain about how hot it is, or you can make the necessary adjustment to be comfortable. The summer day is not going to change; you have to adjust in order to make it through the day with reasonable success. It boils down to a decision of the will.

The same is true of the seasons of our lives. They always come and go. But some seem to last forever, while others pass quickly, and we are able to say that we had a short winter, or that "summer was gone before it began." In God's grace, we are given only what we can handle. And nothing that we are going through is new to God. In fact, it is not even new to man. God has been in this business a long time, and He knows exactly what we need and how much of any given season is enough. That's why it is so important to make the best use of our time, no matter where we find ourselves. A writer long ago said,

This I recall to my mind,
Therefore have I hope.

Through the Lord's mercies
    we are not consumed,
Because His compassions fail not.
They are new every morning;
Great is Your faithfulness.
                —LAMENTATIONS 3:21–23

SUBMITTING TO OUR SEASONS

Esther was a woman of intelligence. She depended on the Holy Spirit to direct her way. If Esther had gone into the king's courts one minute earlier than the appointed time she could have caused great harm to herself and to her people. Everything has a time and season. The more time you spend in God's presence and in His Word, the more pleasing you will be in the King's sight and the more requests you will get answered (Esther 5:3–8).

When the king saw Esther, she was beautiful and perfectly prepared for him (Esther 5:1–2). When the Lord looks at you or me, what does He see? Does He see someone He can use? Does He see someone who is presentable? Does He see someone in whom His seeds of calling are taking root and beginning to grow?

When I think about women and their calling, I am often reminded of the Proverbs 31 women. Now this lady is hard for us to identify with because she just seems too good to be true. She's more like a fairy-tale heroine than a Bible story character. Is it really possible to have a life that falls in place to such a degree? I believe that it is indeed possible, particularly today when women's opportunities are so varied. I am sure the Proverbs 31 woman had her challenges, but she charged ahead in the principles of the Word and she carried on with confidence in the Word. She was an educated, healthy businesswoman who had the gift of philanthropy.

Yet in spite of her thick résumé, she took care of her home first. Her husband could trust her because she was a woman of wisdom. All of her abilities and gifts were put to work, she was fulfilled, and her husband was known in the gates of the city as a community leader. Be careful as you bring home the bacon and fry it up in a pan, that you also wash the pan—that is all part of being a supernatural woman. This godly woman never gave up her home for the marketplace. With God's help, she was able to accomplish everything she wanted to do and live a full life without compromise.

God will not rob us of what He has appointed us to accomplish. He is the One who threw the stars in space; so just maybe He knows how to take care of you and me! He feeds the sparrows; not a single one drops to the ground without His knowledge (Matthew 10:29). A sparrow is worth less than a penny, but our value is much more because we cost Him His life.

What is God calling you to do? To be? Are you avoiding something He's asking you to accomplish? Or are you simply not sure of what He wants? God told the Jews living in the wilderness, "I will lead you with a cloud by day and fire by night" (Exodus 13:21). As your life unfolds, you will get clear direction from the Lord as to what He needs you to do. But He leaves you with a choice. You can decide to pitch a tent, always with the mind-set of folding and moving. Or you can pitch a tent saying, "Hey, I like it here. The Lord couldn't *literally* mean for me to move." I'm sure that's a temptation the Israeli women faced.

Whatever your season, whatever your call, please don't be willful. And don't try to do anything in your own power. His strength is made perfect in your weakness (2 Corinthians 12:9). It's true that these aren't popular ideas in our culture. Listening to God, waiting for His call, allowing Him to be your strength, and choosing to fulfill your season can put you in a lonely position. However, nothing is more rewarding than being in God's will and experiencing His peace.

In order to accomplish the things God has planned for you, you have to be in His Word and in fellowship with His people. And if we are wise, each of us also needs a mentor who is wise in the ways of the Lord. Each of us needs a Mordecai or a Naomi or a Miriam in our life to encourage us when God's call comes, because His call doesn't always look or feel great. Sometimes it is the last thing we want it to be. For example, I grew up in a cultured environment and some of the lessons of my youth about manners and propriety were not at all pleasant for me.

I could never have imagined when I first met my husband that I would be thrust into situations all around the world in which I would need the social graces I had been taught. But in God's sovereign plan, He determined that my foundational training would help touch the world for Jesus Christ. Since that time, God has used my upbringing to complement Tony in many ways. As we have opportunity to travel, I am able to assist Tony in relating to the different cultures we encounter.

Another example of God's calling and instruction in my life took place during a summer camping experience when I was fifteen years old. I directly heard from Him, saying, "Follow me." I remember walking down the aisle saying yes to the Lord but with a whole lot of stipulations.

"Yes, I'll follow You . . . but I don't want to be a missionary."

"Yes, I'll follow You . . . but I'll *never* be a pastor's wife."

Be careful never to say "Never." The Lord has a sense of humor.

The call means that there is a divine purpose for your life that is bigger than you are. Esther's purpose was to save a nation. My purpose is to be a wife—yes, a pastor's wife—to Tony Evans. How tragic it would be for us to settle for a mundane life that never makes the most of our gifts, talents, and interests.

God showed me at fifteen that He had a purpose for my life. I let the Lord know that I was available but scared. Despite all my worries, He took the little seed of faith I carried down that aisle, planted it in good soil, and began the Season of Seed-Planting in my life.

What about you? Have you heard and answered His call? Are the things He's asking you to do too big, too unfamiliar? You have a choice. You can follow the example of Esther, obeying, listening to her mentors, believing in the calling she had among her people. Or you can resist Him, questioning the "senseless" orders He seems to have given.

I hope you'll say yes when He says, "Follow me." The road won't always be easy, but He will never leave you or forsake you. And as you step into the Season of Seed-Planting, He will not be silent. He has promised, as you move through the seasons of your life, that . . .

Your ears shall hear a word behind you, saying,
"This is the way, walk in it,"
Whenever you turn to the right hand
Or whenever you turn to the left.

—ISAIAH 30:21

CHAPTER TWO

The Commitment

✄

So it was . . .
that Esther also was taken to the king's palace,
into the care of Hegai the custodian of the women.

—ESTHER 2:8

As a child growing up, I knew that our family had few worldly goods, but we had a healthy, disciplined home life. Like most young people, I didn't always like the discipline, but I saw and respected the good example set by my parents and their friends.

In those years of growth and development, I didn't realize it, but the Lord had planted another seed in my heart—the seed of commitment. And before I even thought about it, it was beginning to sprout. I began to pray that God would send me a husband who was called by Him and dedicated to His service. I was looking for a man who was committed to God, someone to whom I could commit myself.

When I was eighteen years old, my father was involved in planning a citywide Christian crusade in our area. As it turned out, I was on the welcoming committee for a young man who was to arrive a few days before the featured evangelist. His job was to make sure all the details were taken care of—he was the "advance man." Just before coming to our city, he had recommitted his life to the Lord for full-time service. He, too, was praying that God would bring a woman into his life who would serve the Lord with him.

The young man's name was Tony Evans.

GUESS WHO'S COMING TO DINNER?

My mother was away from home at the time of Tony's visit, so it was up to me to entertain our family's special guest. My memory of Tony Evans's visit to our home centers on my concern that he would enjoy the meal and feel comfortable.

Tony's memory is *Oh my goodness! What a mama-a-jamma—and she can also cook!* He was especially captivated, since the dinner menu that night included fried chicken.

He and I talked a little while before dinner. After dinner, we talked a little more. As far as I was concerned, this was all a part of being hospitable. However, I was soon impressed with Tony's story about how God had moved in his life and the direction in which He was leading him. I also got a chance to hear him practice and preach his first sermon.

Tony and I continued to share and minister together at the crusade, and as hours turned into days, we found ourselves falling in love. To make a long story short, two years later we were married. Tony was in his second year of college, so I joined him in Atlanta and attended Bible college with him. We started a Bible study in Greenville, South Carolina, on the weekends. During those early months of marriage one of his college professors suggested, "Tony, you should apply to Dallas Seminary."

We had already made plans for him to attend another seminary. However, this professor said something that got our attention, especially in light of our grim financial circumstances. He said, "Tony, fill out the application, and I'll pay the registration fees." That was a turning point in our journey. Eventually, we chose Dallas because it provided a better climate for Tony's asthma. And so it was that in 1976 we drove with our two-month-old daughter Chrystal to Texas so that Tony could attend seminary there.

THE CALL TO COMMITMENT

Our move to Dallas was anything but easy. I'll share more about those early days in the next chapters. But I quickly learned something there about God's purposes: Only those who are *committed* to God's purpose will come to know, understand, and experience that purpose. God will only use us to the degree that He can trust us. Commitment—which follows our response to His call to salvation— is a commitment to follow Him, not only as Savior, but as Lord. We commit ourselves to become His disciples. And through discipleship we commit ourselves to God's purpose. Then, as we learn to follow Him, listen to Him, and obey Him, He reveals to us our gifts, talents, and opportunities.

God has given to us the wherewithal to fulfill His kingdom program for us, just as He equipped Esther with what she needed to fulfill His purpose for her life. In fact, Queen Esther's life was a bit like my own. Again, although her Jewish community wasn't wealthy, they also shared strong family ties, godly teaching, and a willingness to serve one another. And, like me, she didn't realize what that specific purpose was until she was committed to being God's woman in the royal court.

A commitment to Jesus and the discipleship process that follows are similar to the education we go through when we are working for an academic degree. Whether it is a two-year associate degree, a four-year bachelor's, or a master's degree, we make the determination that we will commit those years—difficult years though they may be—to the educational process. And as we go through a degree program, there are demanding times, some of them almost unbearable. But we hang in there anyway because there is a goal to accomplish. We change our focus. We say, "I have a purpose in mind."

The same is true with our commitment to what the Lord has called us to do. Whether you are in a top executive role or are filling the double role of a single parent—whatever your status may be at this time—you have been placed where you are "for such a time as this." Eventually, this season will pass and you will be ready for another time, another level of service.

I recently received a call from a single mom. She said, "My boss wants me to come in at 7:30 A.M. and work through lunch to get some projects done. What should I do?"

"What are the benefits of working there?" I asked my friend.

"Well, there are some really good opportunities if you look at the big picture," she explained. "In four years, I will be vested with the company; then I can take a sabbatical with my child. After that, I can consider other employment opportunities. Meanwhile, they are good to me salary-wise, and I get a bonus every year."

"So if you keep your commitment to this job, you'll eventually be at the level you're trying to reach?"

"That's right," she agreed.

My advice to this hardworking single parent was to adjust her lifestyle for this particular season in her life. "If you focus in on your goal, you can make it," I encouraged her. "You'll have to curtail your evening activities so that you can go to bed early and rise early with your child to be at work on time. For the next four years, limit your child's activities to Saturday, so you can have a full day and a long evening together." I made some other suggestions about how she and her child could reschedule their lives to accommodate a season of hard work.

My friend's ultimate goal is to have a flexible schedule so that she can be more available in her child's life. That will come in time, after she has learned all she can from her job. Meanwhile, she can enjoy the benefits, which will help her prepare to establish her own business. Her commitment to a better future requires much of her today, but it promises greater opportunities tomorrow.

And just as our earthly lives require discipline, diligence, and determination, a committed spiritual life requires the same, plus full dependence on Him. We must get to know Him and the power of His resurrection. Only then will we be able to face the demands in our own lives. Only then will we be able to deal with our fears. Esther feared going in to the king; she feared for her life. At first, Esther even allowed fear to obscure her divine perspective. Like us, she was faced with a spiritual battle.

If we are believers, our commitments will always be vulnerable to the opinions of the world, the temptations of the flesh, and the wiles of the devil. However, when it comes to spiritual battles, God's Word makes clear who is in charge of the outcome:

> *Every spirit that does not confess that Jesus Christ has come in the flesh is not of God. And this is the spirit of the Antichrist, which you have heard was coming, and is now already in the world. You are of God, little children, and have overcome them, because He who is in you is greater than he who is in the world.* (1 John 4:3–4)

Commitment involves taking risks, and risks reveal the power of God. Once you've seen the awesome power of God at work in your life, never again will you doubt His capability to help you. Only after you've taken a risk and He has seen you through will you know if your "Amens" on Sunday really work on Monday. Because what He instructs you to do is not always comfortable. In fact, chances are it might be the last thing you "feel" like doing.

COMMIT TO WHAT'S RIGHT, NOT TO WHAT'S POPULAR

Esther was quite content enjoying the benefits of being queen. She wasn't the least bit anxious to give all that up—much less her life —for no good reason. In fact, she had to be reminded of why she was in the palace before she was willing to step out in faith and into the king's presence.

The Christian life is a walk of faith, and faith is "the substance of things hoped for, the evidence of things not seen" (Hebrews 11:1). Through the process of what she went through by faith, Esther eventually saw the reality of God's power, and she learned to trust Him. Her faith became sight. As Andraé Crouch wrote,

> *Through it all*
> *Through it all*
> *Oh I've learned to trust in Jesus . . .*
> *Through it all*
> *I've learned to depend upon His Word.*

When Mordecai told Esther of the Jews' plight at the hand of Haman, she was understandably afraid. Satan is always ready to bring fear into our lives. Esther was afraid of many things—the king's disapproval, the loss of her life, the extermination of her people. Those weren't unrealistic fears. Any of us can lose face, lose friends, lose our place in society when we choose to do what is right, not what is popular. When we take a stand that is painful and we feel all alone, we have to take a deep breath, stand firm in the strength of the Lord, and remind ourselves, "He who is in you is greater than he who is in the world" (1 John 4:4).

I have experienced many lonely times when standing firm over a particular point. I can remember times when I walked into church feeling very much alone because of issues related to my children.

Early in our marriage, Tony and I made a commitment to each other and to God that I would stay home until our kids were ready for school. That amounted to more than fifteen years of being at home. And that wasn't easy. As Tony left for seminary everyday, and later on for his office, I wanted to follow him, with my briefcase in hand. What kept me from working outside the home? Why was I faithful to my call, my commitment? I would say the same words my mother said: "For the Lord's Name's Sake."

I knew God had called me into His service, too. I knew it at age fifteen. But there I was, with little children, feeling alone and isolated. Then one day the Lord reminded me that my four children were my congregation, and my ministry was to raise and instill principles in them. I was using my abilities to manage this ministry. It was a tough time, but I decided to make the best of my present season. It was a choice I had to make, and I made it.

Because I had a higher calling, I knew I would have to give an account for what I did with the gifts God had entrusted to me. So I walked with that confidence and the encouragement of my mentors —my mom and my sister—that I was doing the right thing. Now as I reflect on those hard times of dealing with small children and with a small, complaining, and demanding congregation, I thank the Lord that He gave me all I needed to stand my ground. And today, as I look at my children, I see the Lord's hand in their lives, and I know that it was worth it all.

SAILING THROUGH THE STORM

Making a commitment does not mean that no storms will come up along the way. In fact, it probably means that they will. But when storms arise, we can look to our source of strength for the sustenance to make it through.

I love the words of the prophet Habakkuk, recorded in his book in chapter 3, verses 17 through 19:

> *Though the fig tree may not blossom,*
> *Nor fruit be on the vines;*
> *Though the labor of the olive may fail,*
> *And the fields yield no food;*
> *Though the flock be cut off from the fold,*
> *And there be no herd in the stalls—*
> *Yet I will rejoice in the Lord,*
> *I will joy in the God of my salvation.*
>
> *The Lord God is my strength;*
> *He will make my feet like deer's feet,*
> *And He will make me walk on my high hills.*

Habakkuk's circumstances were certainly gloomy, but in spite of the realities, he decided to rejoice in and trust an all-knowing God. Then or now, that is true commitment.

When our commitments lead us into storms, if we want to have Resurrection Power for Today, we have to put three principles to work: R.P.T.—Rejoice, Pray, Trust. And we have to speak the Word of God into the situation. In Matthew 4, during His temptation, Jesus—who wrote the Word—used the Word on Satan, and Satan had to flee. If the One who wrote the Word found it necessary to use the Word, how much more should you and I put the Word to work in our own lives?

And in order to use the Word, you have to know the Word.

Whatever the problem you face, whether at home or at work, with family or friends, or even enemies,

- *Rejoice* that God has allowed you to trust Him.
- *Pray* the blood of Jesus on whatever satanic powers may be at work. Pray without ceasing. You can't always close your eyes, but you can pray without ceasing. It is your spiritual oxygen. You can't stop breathing physically and expect to live—no oxygen produces death. In a similar sense, prayer keeps spiritual oxygen supplied to the body to keep it productive and alive.
- *Trust* the One you pray to because you are praying in the name of the same Jesus who said to the sea, "Peace, be still!"

When the disciples thought they were about to lose their lives because of a sudden storm, they cried out in panic. And Jesus rescued them. When the winds and waves come crashing into your life, what is the first thing you should do? Should you compare your situation to those of others? Should you blame everybody you can think of? Or should you look up and say, "Master, do You not care that we perish?" Our Lord is never asleep. It's when the billows of life get too strong and too powerful—and now and then they will—that we sometimes forget what a mighty God we serve.

I got a chance to see the Lake of Galilee on a recent visit to Israel. It was one of my favorite spots because it brought to life for me the reality of Jesus and the disciples in the boat. On a clear day in Galilee you can stand on one side of the bank and clearly see the other side. However, when heavy winds howl and the clouds roll in, you can't see the other side at all. Even though you know it's there, it's completely out of sight.

In our panic, we try to paddle and steer our own boats. Sometimes we even jump out of the boat the Master is in, thinking we have a better plan. The disciples were in deep fear, but they managed to stay on board and finally decided to wake Him up. Let's commit ourselves to doing the same. Let's stay on board, stay on course, and tell Jesus we've had enough.

Once we "wake Him up," God is such a wonderful Father, He'll calm the sea and we'll be able to see the other side. He will say, "Peace, be still!" and even the winds and the sea will obey Him. Cry out to Him; let Him know you cannot bear your burdens any longer. Never forget that the God who led you into this challenge is the same God who has all the power necessary to quiet the storm. He is the resurrected Son of God, and He can meet all of your needs according to His riches in glory.

"He Didn't Bring Us Here to Leave Us"

Once Tony and I made the decision to move to Dallas, everything wasn't suddenly ideal. We ran into storms of every size and severity. It took faith and belief that God wanted us there, because it was a tough time for us. In fact, if we hadn't been committed to God and to His plan, we never would have made it through.

We had a lot of lack financially and materially, but we had this inner confidence that God had directed us. So we held on to our commitment in spite of the circumstances. We did what we could for ourselves, but we stayed open to His will. And when challenges arose, we knew for sure that we were right where we belonged because Dallas had never been in our plans to begin with. Although it was difficult, I could always say, "We're children of the King, and the King has good plans for us and for our future. He didn't bring us here to leave us."

Like Esther, like me, like every woman who answers God's call and commits herself to His service, you are part of His royal court. When you trusted Jesus Christ as personal Savior, you were accepted into His royal family. No matter what season of life you are in, you have royal blood flowing through your veins.

Maximize the time you have on God's earth as a royal heir to the throne. Live to the fullest in your season. From cradle to grave, each period in life has its benefits and sacrifices. Learn all you can as you go. Then you'll be able to move gracefully into your next season with a sense of accomplishment as you look back and a sense of anticipation as you look ahead. You are the beloved daughter of a great and mighty King.

Faith to Fly

Tony laughs about my faith in flying. On several occasions, because his schedule didn't allow him to travel on a commercial airline, groups have sent private planes for Tony to transport him to speaking engagements. I generally don't travel with him on those occasions because I am not particularly fond of flying in small planes.

On one occasion I was invited to fly with him to Iowa on a commercial airline, and I was more than happy to say yes. Then plans changed. The host church offered to arrange a private plane and pilot for us.

One pilot, not two, I thought. My decision changed. "Sorry, I can't make it," I smiled.

Then things got changed around again. Suddenly we were back on the large commercial plane. My decision changed, too. I said yes.

My decision was based on my faith in the plane; my faith depended on the size of the plane.

For me to have faith in a plane, it has to be a big plane. For any of us to have faith in God, we must have a big God. We can only get an idea about how big God is when we get to know Him through His Word. And we can only prove to ourselves how big He really is as we make it through all the challenges He brings into our lives.

No one wants to make a commitment to something unsafe, untrustworthy, or unreliable. But God isn't asking us to do that. When He plants the seed of commitment in our hearts, He makes a deep and abiding promise to us:

> *"Fear not, for I am with you;*
> *Be not dismayed, for I am your God.*
> *I will strengthen you,*
> *Yes, I will help you,*
> *I will uphold you with My righteous right hand."*
> —ISAIAH 41:10

Christian Communion

Now the young woman pleased [Hegai],
and she obtained his favor;
so he readily gave beauty preparations to her.
—ESTHER 2:9

*S*eminary was an exciting but challenging time. Tony and I knew in our hearts that God had called us to Dallas, but the realities we faced every day were affirming the opposite. With a full seminary load, Tony could not work full-time, so I had to make up the difference. That meant taking Chrystal to a baby-sitter every morning. Eventually, that routine got to be a waste of our resources because Chrystal became ill and had to be taken to the doctor's office on a regular basis. Naturally, that lessened the amount of money I was able to bring home.

It was at this point that Tony and I decided to keep the commitment we had made while we were dating, that I would stay home with our kids until they were school-age. We began to think that maybe God had included Tony's seminary years in that commitment. And as we prayed and waited, we saw Him provide for us over and over again. Nonetheless, it was a difficult time for me because my whole world revolved around Chrystal and Tony and books.

The seminary provided some outlets for the wives of students, and I took advantage of them all. There were seminary wives' fellowships, potlucks in seminary professors' homes, and other social opportunities. But there were some painful experiences, too. We were turned down for a decent apartment dwelling because we were African-American. We were made to feel unwelcome in a local Bible church. And from time to time, we were excluded from various social gatherings for the same reason.

All this took place in the 1970s, not many years after the civil rights struggles of the '60s. Dallas was a very conservative city, and Tony was only the fourth African-American to attend Dallas Theological Seminary. But despite some of the racial inequalities we faced, God, in His grace, brought many people into our lives who genuinely cared about us.

FINDING HIM IN THE SECRET PLACE

Because of the commitment we made to child rearing, we lived on a tight budget. That meant we had to do something that was very difficult for me—we got both food and clothing from St. Luke's closet, a resource for needy families. I had a hard time with that. Although I had been raised in a modest family, we never had to depend on anyone outside of our home for help.

During those lean years, I learned what trusting God really meant. We had to trust Him for daily sustenance. I learned firsthand what the psalmist meant when he wrote, "I have been young, and now am old; yet I have not seen the righteous forsaken, nor his descendants begging bread" (Psalm 37:25). I had to swallow my pride and shop in a store of castaway clothes. But I sure looked good.

Right now as I am typing this, there are some needs in our lives that will have to be met on schedule. The lessons I learned during those seminary years make it possible for me to say that I can truly trust in the Lord. The same God who met our needs yesterday and meets them today will do so tomorrow.

I also learned to make the most out of what we had: ground beef, ground beef, ground beef, and ground beef. I cooked it in as many variations as I could imagine, but it was still ground beef. Chicken was a delicacy. Steak? It never happened in seminary.

Of all the things I learned, however, the most important lesson was the importance of a private relationship with God. He taught me, day after day, that my communion with Him is the source from which all my strength flows. The Scripture tells us,

He who dwells in the secret place of the Most High
Shall abide under the shadow of the Almighty.

—PSALM 91:1

That's the same secret place Jesus was talking about when He said,

"When you pray, go into your room, and when you have shut your door, pray to your Father who is in the secret place; and your Father who sees in secret will reward you openly." (Matthew 6:6)

Communion is intimate fellowship and rapport with Jesus Christ. We have to have intimate fellowship. At the cross we were bought with a price, and at the point of salvation we were introduced to the One who bought us. But to know and understand all the benefits of the price paid, we have to read the directions and get to know the Manufacturer really well.

We have to fill out the lifetime warranty form so that we can access the Manufacturer anytime there is a need. We have to find out how to call on the One who bought us and how to read His directions for a godly life. We have to build an ongoing relationship with Jesus Christ.

If we want to reap the full benefits of our life in Christ, we have to know Him. We can only know Him by spending time in His Word, in prayer, and in meditation. Communication with Him does not happen by chance. It is a decision of the will.

"THEY THAT WAIT ON THE LORD . . ."

There are seasons in life where it seems that we are at a standstill. The seminary years were like that for me. In such a season time feels like it is moving slowly or not at all. Whatever we're passing through, we wait for change—we wait for young children to grow, wait to find a new job, wait until the discomforts of menopause pass, or wait out illness with our parents—and we feel stuck. What should we do? Should we generate more activity, or should we look into Jesus' face and trust Him to make the path clear? Although stirring things up may momentarily relieve our frustration, as God's children, we are supposed to allow Him to work out every aspect of our lives—*in His time.*

During a season when we are awaiting change, it is easy for Satan to get our attention because we are not used to being quiet. We go through the motions of mundane daily activity, we find nothing to do that is stimulating, and we question God. Meanwhile, the world screams, "You must do this; you must do that. God never intended for you to be still at this time. If you continue to wait, the world will pass you by."

The Lord has a different message. In Isaiah we read:

> *But those who wait on the Lord*
> *Shall renew their strength;*
> *They shall mount up with wings like eagles,*
> *They shall run and not be weary,*
> *They shall walk and not faint.*
>
> —ISAIAH 40:31

To wait on the Lord means to be patient and quiet while He is at work. We wait in His presence in that secret place to which He has called us. In that place He will help us understand the importance of patience, the value of rest in Him, and the eternal significance of staying in the center of His will.

There is nothing wrong with wanting more out of life, but there is everything wrong in wanting more simply to gratify ourselves: "More for more's sake." You always know when more is too much because it invariably takes you outside of the will of God. How do we know when we are outside the will of God? We know when we start manipulating the Scriptures, trying to interpret them according to our likes and dislikes. We know when we forge forward, determined to have our way.

I love the words of Jesus: "If you abide in Me, and My words abide in you, you will ask what you desire, and it shall be done for you" (John 15:7). What a great promise is ours when we know Him and commune with Him! If we abide in Him, our desires and thoughts are only in our hearts because He's the One who placed them there in the first place. Now that's communion.

But it isn't always easy. Communion with Him in prayer and in the Word are sometimes the last things we want to do or are motivated to do. Why? Because Satan knows how powerful we can be when we wait on the Lord and have our strength renewed. He is well aware that by abiding in Jesus believers have enough power to live the Christian life as overcomers. And that's the last thing our enemy wants.

You may need to lessen your exposure to television, secular magazines, and talk radio and refuse to allow your mind to be influenced by the thousands of ungodly messages that bombard us every day. The world system wants us to believe that we are self-sustaining beings who don't need anyone. But John 15:5 says we can do nothing without Him. Who is telling us the truth? The more time we spend with Jesus, the more we come to understand why we need Him every hour of every day.

PRAISE IN THE MIDST OF PAIN

One day, one of the Dallas Seminary professors' wives invited me to attend a Bible study she was teaching, and baby-sitting was provided. I attended with great excitement, only to bump into the reality of being once again unwelcome. The group was made up of very wealthy Anglo women; however, I will never forget how careful my hostess was to make sure I was included. She even bought me the books to study from. I have one of those books on my mantle today—it reminds me of the grace of God that I saw so beautifully expressed in that lady's life.

Although I never felt welcome during those early years at that Bible study, I learned a lot about love and perseverance. I learned that regardless of the obstacles in life, we have to press on with what God has instructed us to do. I remember one particular time when our Bible study group was invited to the home of one of the members for a prayer ministry. I was welcomed at the door, but that was all. The hostess was visibly annoyed that I was there. The rest of the women ignored me.

Does God feel our heartaches? Is He aware of our rejections, adversities, and loneliness? When we pour out our hearts to Him, does He really listen? Does He really hear? Does He really answer our prayers? Over twenty-seven years later that same group, now under new leadership, invited me to sit on their board. I was also asked to share in music at one of their banquets. "You prepare a table before me in the presence of my enemies," the psalmist said (Psalm 23:5).

God's intervention in our lives is grounds for praise, but we're supposed to praise Him even when we're still waiting and watching and wondering. Another psalm—Psalm 150—talks about true praise: "Let everything that has breath praise the Lord" (v. 6). It's so important for us to give Him thanks, even when, in our humble opinion, there is nothing to thank Him for. I decided to develop that discipline in my life during our dark days as we faced so many challenges as a family. I told the Lord, "I can't fix a thing. All I can do is learn to find something in these gloomy days to thank You for."

Trust me, it was hard for me, because I just don't naturally see what is not there. But I developed the discipline of thanking Him for the fact that I was breathing, for my car, for each bright day, for my children's lives, and for our health. I worked at it until it became a way of life for me.

I have a history with Him now. I know firsthand that He can make a way out of no way. I know that He is able to carry me through the pain. I know that He will not give me more than I can bear, even though I am crying out, "God, this is unbearable!"

Somehow, I have learned to pull myself together and cling to the truth of His Word even when I don't have the necessary correlating feeling. With the constant persistence of this discipline, it becomes a way of life. Not succumbing to the lies of the devil is a choice. Listening to the Lord is a choice, too: He speaks in a still, small voice and we have to be still enough to hear Him speak.

I can assure you from my own experience that we need to spend time alone with the Lord. We spend all kinds of time trying to accomplish other things. We're patient and diligent and persistent. But when it comes to the divine, eternal plan for our lives, we want instant answers and instant gratification.

In one sense, I understand that, for we live in a world that insists on instant-this and drive-through-that. However, in order to grow in grace, we must be alone. We must be patient. We must wait on the Lord. We must abide in Him. One single quiet hour of prayer will often make more progress than several days of communion with others. It is in the desert that the dew falls freshest and the air is purest.

But I also sincerely believe that other believers play a vital role in our lives. People who pray with us, mentor us, love us, and speak truth to us are part of God's plan for the body of Christ. We are not meant to remain alone. But don't mistake a lunch with a gossiping group of women for true communion. And don't exchange social time with others for quiet, reflective one-on-one communion with Him. If we spent just half as much time with God as we spend with friends, we might be able to handle the seasons of our lives.

MAKING COMMUNION PART OF OUR LIVES

Psalm 1:1–3 says:

> *Blessed is the man*
> > *Who walks not in the counsel*
> > > *of the ungodly,*
> > *Nor stands in the path of sinners,*
> > *Nor sits in the seat of the scornful;*
> *But his delight is in the law of the Lord,*
> > *And in His law he meditates day and night.*
> *He shall be like a tree*
> > *Planted by the rivers of water,*
> > *That brings forth its fruit in its season,*

Whose leaf also shall not wither;
And whatever he does shall prosper.

In the privacy of the secret place, God is doing some deep work inside you. He is allowing His Spirit to flow through you. He is digging out irrigation channels so that His truth can penetrate your roots. Stand still. Let those rivers of water run, pool, and store up in your root system so that you can flourish in the next season—the Season of Growth.

Esther's confidence grew during the time she spent alone. We'll talk more about her time of preparation in chapter 6. But suffice it to say for now if she had gone in too early to see the king, she would not have been presentable for a hearing. She would have displeased him. He would not have heard her appeal for help.

The Persian king had a rule requiring twelve months of preparation before a woman could enter his presence. The King of the universe has also set a specific time period for communion with Him in each of our lives before we are adequately prepared for His purposes. Did it ever occur to you that perhaps God will keep you from entering your next season, perhaps even from finding your life's partner, until you learn to first give Him your full, wholehearted attention?

Spending time with the Lord is not an easy task in this frenetic world with all its hectic schedules and relentless demands. We need to schedule in our God-time, or we will never get it done—because nothing takes top priority over our Top Priority. If you have to be in the office really early, schedule your time with the Lord on your first break or during lunchtime. If you are at home, schedule it as soon as the kids leave for school. If you are an early riser, schedule it before you get on the treadmill. If you are a late-nighter, and you are positive you won't fall asleep in the middle of your prayers, then schedule it after everyone else has gone to sleep.

Having personal devotions and having devotions with our children are indispensable. Deuteronomy 6:6–9 tells us, regarding the words the Lord speaks, "These words which I command you today shall be in your heart; you shall teach them diligently to your children, and shall talk of them when you sit in your house, when you walk by the way, when you lie down, and when you rise up. You shall bind them as a sign on your hand, and they shall be as frontlets between your eyes. You shall write them on the doorposts of your house and on your gates."

It is helpful when we place Scripture all around our homes. We can frame verses and hang them on walls. We can purchase them on little memorization cards. We can stick Scripture magnets on the refrigerator. We should do whatever it takes to saturate our sons and daughters with His Word.

As a single parent, it is possible to raise a child in the fear and admonition of the Lord. Mordecai did that with Esther. And Mordecai also had a community of people involved in Esther's life. We need the community of believers to be involved (not take our place) in our lives and in the lives of our children. But it all begins in personal communion as we develop intimacy with God.

COMMUNION WITH THE GOD WHO SEES AND ANSWERS

During our seminary days in Dallas, Tony and I made up our minds that we would rise above the many difficult situations and move forward in spite of them. It was never easy. In fact, one terrible day the lack of money and the isolation just became unbearable for me.

"I just don't know," I told Tony, my eyes overflowing with tears, "if I can go on. I really don't know."

By then, we had two children and were living in a part of town where no relationships were possible.

Tony and I had our devotions together, as usual, before he left for school. I was crying inconsolably, and asking, "Why can't the Lord just provide for us? Why doesn't He help us?"

Tony was heartbroken. After devotions, after encouraging me as much as he could, he said, "I'm going to trust the Lord to meet our needs. How much do we need to get through another month?"

"Five hundred dollars," I told him, still in tears.

That was a lot of money in those days. He said, "I am going to trust God to provide five hundred dollars for us today. If He doesn't, then I'll assume that He wants me to drop out of seminary for at least a year to get my family settled."

With that he left. As was his habit, once he got to the seminary he went to the mailbox to check the mail. He ripped open an envelope that bore no return address. There in the mail was $500 in cash sent by an anonymous donor.

Tony called me immediately, exulting in what God had done. I was awestruck. We never again challenged God's sovereignty or His call for us to be in seminary. Although those were times of stretching, times of struggling, I learned to trust God for real. I'd always known in my head that God is a bridge over troubled waters. I could speak the language. But never before had I experienced such power for myself. Seminary taught me what communion with God really is.

And what about your life? If you know the Lord, you and I serve the same mighty God. Are you making sure communion with God is the Top Priority in your life? Are you seeing His mighty hand at work in your circumstances? It may take on a different form and shape for you than it did for me, but please be sure that God's intervention is a regular part of your Christian walk. And it all starts with communion. Think about this promise:

"Call to Me, and I will answer you,
and show you great and mighty things,
which you do not know."
—JEREMIAH 33:3

PART
TWO

The
Season
of
Growth

CHAPTER
FOUR

Obedience

*So Esther was taken to King Ahasuerus, into his royal palace,
in the tenth month, which is the month of Tebeth,
in the seventh year of his reign.
The king loved Esther more than all the other women,
and she obtained grace and favor in his sight
more than all the virgins;
so he set the royal crown upon her head
and made her queen instead of Vashti.*

—ESTHER 2:16–17

Have you ever planted a rosebush? At first, rosebushes are scrawny, thorny sticks that don't show much promise. You dig a hole in the garden, stick the plant in the ground, and look at the little cardboard tag, trying to convince yourself that such a pathetic twig will actually bear lovely blossoms. But after a few seasons of careful irrigation, fertilizing, and pruning, one day you wake up to see a lush, leafy plant covered in vividly colored, fragrant roses.

In nature, growth comes as the result of health and nourishment. Plants and animals have to follow the laws of the Creator in order to grow healthy, strong, and beautiful. The same principles apply to spiritual growth. As Christian women, our spiritual growth depends on our health, and our health depends on our obedience to God's rules. We can never bloom into our full potential unless we are obedient.

As long as we're alive, we never stop growing. But the Season of Growth is a special time of our lives when we go through an intense process of obedience, service, and preparation for the future God has designed us for. My Season of Growth took place in the early years of my marriage to Tony, during his time of seminary and the surprising years that followed.

From the time I first met Tony, he had told me that he was going to be an evangelist. So once we decided to marry, I tried to prepare myself mentally for the fact that he would be gone quite a bit. Then, the last year of seminary, a professor challenged him with the idea of starting a church. When Tony arrived home one day, he was bursting with this bright idea. "I think maybe God wants us to start our own church. I'll be the pastor . . ."

I thought he was kidding.

He wasn't.

My response spilled out in pools of tears. I cried because I was horrified to think that I would have to play the one role I dreaded more than any other. I would have to be *that lady*—the pastor's wife. But tears or no tears, in 1976 we started Oak Cliff Bible Fellowship with ten people in our home, and my worst fears were realized. I thought I had to be all things to all people—and everyone else seemed to think so, too. The expectation was that I should be able to teach, play the piano, and take care of everyone's children. And I was to do it with a smile.

I did a lot of soul-searching in those early days. And after much reflection on what God had first called me to do at fifteen, I began to see that no matter what role I played, He wanted me to be myself and to use the gifts He had given me. Naturally, my gifts might not get the approval of everyone, but I would eventually have to answer to God for what I did with those gifts.

Of course all that sounds great now, and it was a great idea even then, but I had to work it out in the reality of daily living. Over two years of trial and error, with Tony's and my sister Elizabeth's help, listening ear, and prayer, I made a decision to accept my calling in life. I read as many books as I could find on this new vocation I was in. One of the better ones was by Ruth Senter, *So You're the Pastor's Wife* (Grand Rapids: Zondervan, 1979). I discovered that I was supposed to be Tony's wife, not the church's wife. Finally, after two years of hoping that Tony would get tired of the church idea, I saw our fellowship begin to grow. I couldn't help but see God's hand in our lives and ministry.

There were several painful times during those ministry days. Yet as I write today it is a dull pain, a bit like childbearing. You always remember the birth of your child, but the memory of the pain lessens as the months and years pass. You can say that it was painful, but you actually don't feel the pain as you reflect upon it.

I can imagine that all the details of Esther's promotion to queen of Persia weren't easy. She had to learn many things about royal protocol. She had to observe a variety of "house rules" to avoid the fate of her predecessor, Vashti. She probably made mistakes and had to be corrected and counseled by Hegai, the keeper of the women. In order for Esther to fulfill God's plan for her life, she had to be obedient to the ways of the Persian culture and to the king's rule over her.

Obedience to God's plan is rarely easy. It often requires us to do the last thing we ever wanted to do. It may mean wrestling with unruly emotions. It may mean overcoming prejudices and preconceived notions. It may mean humbling ourselves before God and pleading with Him for the strength to carry on. But if we are to grow into the women He has in mind for us to be, we have to obey.

Obedience as Daughters of the King

Fortunately, most of us don't experience the demands faced by a young queen in a foreign court. But we are all daughters of a heavenly King, and we have to learn to submit to Him, His kingdom, and His ways.

The first way we do this is by being obedient to the King's written Word. In the previous chapter we talked about having communion with Him, spending time alone with the Lord, and getting to know Him. This is essential to our obedience, for unless we know what His Word says, how can we obey it? The Bible is His royal edict to us.

God's Word also admonishes us to obey those in God-given authority over us (unless they require us to act in a way that contradicts His written Word). Just as earthly kings have a hierarchy surrounding them, He has set up an order of authority and He requires us—men, women, and children—to fit into that flow of authority. One of the challenges facing women today is the issue of submission. And yet God requires the submission of every one of His children: to Him first, then to political orders, to police, to professors, to pastors, to parents and—yes, ladies—to husbands (Ephesians 5:22).

We are also called to obey the still, small voice within us. Sometimes we talk about the voice of our conscience. Other times, we say that the Holy Spirit has spoken to our hearts. Either way, we can test the inner voice we hear by making sure that it agrees with God's written Word. If it doesn't, it's probably our own voice trying to tell us to follow our own will. That's not the voice we should obey!

OBEDIENCE—OUR LOVE LANGUAGE TO GOD

In the Old Testament, animal sacrifices were required of the people in order to allow them into God's Presence. Yet we learn from Scripture that there was one thing more important to God than any animal sacrifice. In 1 Samuel 15:22, God's Word tells us, "Behold, to obey is better than sacrifice, and to heed [listen and obey] than the fat of rams." Obedience is better than sacrifice.

In the New Testament, Jesus made the same point even more clearly. He simply said, "If you love Me, keep My commandments" (John 14:15).

How do you feel when your children do things they know you don't approve of? Don't you somehow feel that their love for you is lacking? Don't you wonder how they can say they love you and then break your heart? Jesus is saying the same thing. He's saying that we shouldn't keep singing, "Oh, how I love Jesus!" and then go out and ignore all His rules. When we love people, we want to please them. The same is true of our love for God.

We also obey God so that we can cooperate with His work within us. Because He loves us, He wants us to be more like Him. So He is "growing" us up in grace. According to Romans 12:1–2, spiritual growth means being "transformed by the renewing of your mind." Obedience means that we are cooperating with the transformation process. As God changes us on the inside, we work together with

Him by making changes in our outward behavior. After years of growth, we discover that our branches are bearing good spiritual fruit. We find that we don't want to keep doing the same old wrong things we used to enjoy. Instead, we delight in doing His will. But we don't reach that point unless we cooperate with God's growth process through obedience.

Because we're human, and therefore flawed by sin, we're never going to get it just right. However, when we disobey, provision has already been made for us. First John 1:9 promises, "If we confess our sins, He is faithful and just to forgive us our sins and to cleanse us from all unrighteousness." That's the good news. The bad news is that when we disobey we often still have to face the consequences of our disobedience even though God has forgiven and cleansed us.

Too Busy to Get to Know Him?

Why do we disobey? Could it be that we are lacking relationship with, respect for, and confidence in the One we should gladly obey? If you ever really get to know Him, I can tell you firsthand that you'll begin to realize the power you received at the point of salvation. But it is Satan's job to keep us so busy that we never take the time to get to know Him.

Think about the familiar story of Martha and Mary found in Luke 10:38–42. The Bible tells us about two sisters who were busy preparing for Jesus' visit. Now I can relate to Martha, because I believe in everything being done decently and in order. If I have invited someone to dinner, especially someone who can raise the dead and heal the sick, I will be in the kitchen for days, just to make sure that everything is perfect and every dish is delicious.

Verse 40 says, "But Martha was distracted with much serving, and she approached Him and said, Lord, do You not care that my sister has left me to serve alone? Therefore tell her to help me."

The key element to notice there is "Do You not care that my sister has *left* me to serve alone?" That question indicates that Mary had also been busy in the kitchen at some point. Later, she must have made a decision to sit at Jesus' feet.

Obedience is a choice. And obedience is not easy. We always have to make a decision to obey in the midst of business, in the midst of opposition. Oftentimes, it is not a popular decision—in this case, Martha was rather upset. When you obey, some people will think you are crazy. You will be disliked. You might even be left all alone. But Mary chose the better part. She spent quality time with her Guest.

To obey the Master seems, sometimes, to make no sense at all. But once we seriously reflect upon who He is and what He can do in our lives, we find a way to make the adjustment. Maybe you have a good, loving relationship with your earthly father. If so, you probably enjoy doing nice things for him. How much more should you want to please your heavenly Father? He has all power. He has a heart full of love for you. And He has your future written into His plans for the universe.

Obeying Is an Expression of Faith

One of the problems we have with obedience is that we don't trust God. Instead, we try to provide for our own needs by disobeying His Word. Is the Lord your Shepherd? Then count on the Good Shepherd to take care of His sheep. If the Lord is your Shepherd, then He will meet all of your needs. You don't have to take care of them yourself through unholy means.

Because the Lord is your Shepherd, you don't have to provide for your financial needs by taking money that doesn't belong to you.

Because the Lord is your Shepherd, you don't have to provide for your love needs by stealing another woman's man.

Because the Lord is your Shepherd, you don't have to provide for your emotional needs by killing your pain with alcohol or drugs.

Because the Lord is your Shepherd, you don't have to provide for your material needs by running up huge debts that you can't handle.

God is trustworthy and holy. He will take care of you in righteous ways. He will give you more than you could ask or think in ways that are in accordance with His Word.

When Esther and Mordecai heard about Haman's plot to destroy the Jewish people, they could not see deliverance, but they had faith in the Deliverer. They didn't plot a murder or try to stir up a military conflict. They had seen God work before, and that gave them the courage to allow His will to be worked out through them. Have you seen God work before? If it gets foggy and you can't see God's hand today, just hang on till tomorrow. As Lamentations says, the Lord's mercies "are new every morning" (Lamentations 3:23). The way will clear and the answer will come because He is faithful.

Don't doubt in the darkness what God has done in the light.

SEASONS OF OBEDIENCE

What season is this for you? What is it that God is asking you to do?

Are you single, and is He asking you to remain pure and holy? Is He telling you to wait for His man and not be unequally yoked to an unbeliever? Is He asking you to spend time with Him, not filling your life with romance novels and magazines telling you how to catch a husband?

Are you a new wife, and is He asking you to submit to your husband? Is He teaching you the disciplines of cooking, cleaning, and caring for your home, maybe while also managing a career outside of the home? Is the Lord calling upon you to learn His ways regarding marriage and family and to leave the world's ways behind?

Are you a mother, wrestling with responsibility and no free time? Is the Lord asking you to sacrifice your gifts and dreams in the marketplace for a season while you bring up your kids? Is He telling you to love your children the way He loves His children—with both mercy and godly discipline? Is He teaching you patience?

Are you in a season when your kids are grown and gone? Is God calling you to serve Him in new ways, to reach out to others, to fulfill the gifts you had to set aside while your children were growing? Is He challenging you to leave your children in His hands and to trust Him to care for them now that you are no longer in control? Is He teaching you to set aside self-pity and to rejoice in Him, despite the aging process?

We can only obey and have confidence in One with whom we have a trusting relationship. God speaks to us constantly, but if we're not familiar with His voice, we will obey our own instead because it will sound better to us than His. Just as He asked me to obey Him and become a pastor's wife, He may ask you to do something you'd rather not do.

Sometimes God has to take us out on the Sea of Galilee and into a storm to show us His power. When the disciples got discouraged, they forgot His promise that they were going to the other side. When life comes billowing in, we often forget what He's said. We may even get mad at Him. We feel so all alone and start thinking about abandoning ship.

Esther wanted to keep quiet; she wanted to abandon ship. I wanted to avoid being *that woman*—the pastor's wife. How many times have you felt like abandoning ship, whether the ship is the children, the marriage, the church, or the job? Have you wanted to abandon ship as you and your parents deal with the maturing process at different levels, yet at the same time? Just maybe He wants you to call on Him and not on your own strengths and abilities, which are not enough to get you through the storms. He certainly didn't give us strengths and abilities so that we would become independent of Him. It bears repeating: Without Him we can do nothing, as John 15:5 reminds us.

The Lord wants us to simply obey, even when the boat is about to sink. Now you have to know Someone really well to believe that in a life-and-death situation, He will show up just in time. Haman thought his plan to kill Mordecai and all the Jewish people was about to become reality. He even had the gallows built. Mordecai was as good as dead. Then God stepped in.

God stepped in because Esther obeyed—but she wasn't alone in her obedience. God provided wise counsel in Mordecai. God prepared the heart of the king. God put the pieces together. Because of Esther's obedience and because of God's intervention, her enemy became her footstool. In fact it got even better—Haman was on his knees begging Esther for his life, and the king mistook his position before the queen as one of seduction. He thought Haman was about to assault the queen, so he hanged Haman on the very gallows Haman had prepared for Mordecai (Esther 7:7–10).

There is a price to pay for obedience, but the rewards are wonderful. "Vengeance is Mine, I will repay" is promised in both the New and Old Testaments (Romans 12:19, which refers to Deuteronomy 32:35). I believe that at the heart of that promise the Lord really means that if you will obey Him, trust Him, and allow Him to do so, He will take care of you.

Deuteronomy 29:29 says, "The secret things belong to the Lord our God, but those things which are revealed belong to us and to our children forever, that we may do all the words of this law." God chooses not to reveal everything to us, but He has revealed some things to us. And a few things we know for sure. He always wants us to remember that He is God. He wants us to submit. He wants us to trust. He wants us to obey Him, just as Jesus did. Jesus had to learn obedience through suffering. And He learned it for us—to teach us and to save us.

Though He was a Son, yet He learned obedience
by the things which He suffered.
And having been perfected, He became the author of
eternal salvation to all who obey Him.
—HEBREWS 5:8–9

CHAPTER FIVE

Service

*Then the king made a great feast, the Feast of Esther,
for all his officials and servants. . . .
When the virgins were gathered together a second time,
Mordecai sat within the king's gate.
Now Esther had not revealed her kindred and her people,
just as Mordecai had charged her.*

—ESTHER 2:18–20

*D*uring Seasons of Growth, we often find ourselves doing things we really didn't plan to do. As we saw in the last chapter, that is often the case when we obey—we don't necessarily enjoy doing it. Obedience doesn't always feel good, and neither does service. Our human nature, which loves to place us in a role of power and glory, thinks we ought to be waited on hand and foot. At the core of our being we want to be pampered, fussed over, and catered to.

As Christians, if we're serious about our faith, we won't get very far with that idea. We have a model to follow who doesn't cut us much slack when it comes to service. Jesus was the Creator of the Universe, the God of all Creation. Yet in Matthew 20:27–28 we read His words, "Whoever desires to be first among you, let him be your slave—just as the Son of Man did not come to be served, but to serve, and to give His life a ransom for many."

In Philippians 2:5–8, we discover more about Jesus' decision to step down into a servant's role, and we are given a challenge to follow in His footsteps.

> *Let this mind be in you, which was also in Christ Jesus, who, being in the form of God, did not consider it robbery to be equal with God, but made Himself of no reputation, taking the form of a servant, and coming in the likeness of men. And being found in appearance as a man, He humbled Himself and became obedient to the point of death, even the death of the cross.*

There's no question about it—if we are going to follow Jesus Christ, we are going to be servants. Our Master washed His friends' feet. Are we greater than He is? He went so far as to die so that others could live. Are we willing to follow Him to the cross?

Unfortunately, even if we say yes we soon learn that the kinds of service in which we are engaged hardly seem as "spiritual" and "glorious" as the things Jesus did. We find ourselves changing diapers, cleaning bathrooms, helping out in the church nursery, balancing the checkbook, and scouring pots and pans. We get caught in a seemingly endless cycle of tasks that have to be redone again and again. How can we find satisfaction or fulfillment in endless, mindless activities like that? Sure, we're called to be servants, but is this what He had in mind?

In fact, every act of service we do is not only what He had in mind, but what He requires of us. And He makes it very clear, according to His Word, who it is we are serving: "Servants, be obedient to those who are your masters according to the flesh, with fear and trembling, in sincerity of heart, as to Christ; not with eyeservice, as men-pleasers, but as servants of Christ, doing the will of God from the heart, with good will doing service, as to the Lord, and not to men" (Ephesians 6:5–7).

Like obedience, service is something we offer up to God as an act of trust and love and worship. We serve because we love—we love Him, and we love those around us. Love, in fact, requires service. We serve our families. We serve our friends. We serve in organizations.

We serve our churches. And as we serve men and women, boys and girls, we are actually serving the Lord.

SERVICE IN THE SEASON OF GROWTH

From age fifteen, I knew that God had given me unique gifts and had called me to serve Him in the areas of business and music. I also knew that when our children were very young, they needed me to be at home with them. But my decision to stay home and serve them didn't come easily.

So many times I talked with Tony about going to work outside the home, especially since my gifts didn't really fit into the scheme of things at the church. I wanted to finish my degree and then work in my field of business administration. I wanted to experience the world of meetings, opportunities, coffee breaks and—perhaps above all else—intelligible conversations. I wanted to leave the repetitive, unrewarding (at that time) care of my little ones to someone else.

But I had both an example and a mentor rolled into one who wasn't going to let that happen: my mother. She had made a major commitment to stay home and invest herself in eight children's lives. And she often reminded me that those four kids of mine were my church. With that in mind, I had to refocus on my ministry.

Every day I left with my briefcase, but it simply went with me from one room to the other. I began to see that I had some important business to attend to. I had been given four very special projects that would have to be seen through to completion. Someone had to instill godly principals in my children's lives, and God let me know that I was the woman for the job.

Now I'm not saying for a minute that it was easy. It wasn't. And if you are raising young children right now, I know how you feel. I know that on some days you just want to get up, get dressed, put on some lipstick, and walk right out the door. Like me, you've probably learned that we have to make decisions with our will, not with our heart.

In a very real sense, I became a servant to my children. And I did it by managing my home like a business. By nature, I'm a manager. I love detail. I love to plan ahead. In those days, I even planned our meals for the week and posted a chart on the refrigerator reminding me of what we were going to eat. God gave me an opportunity to see during that season of my life that "little is much if He is in it." I can still go to the refrigerator and make a whole meal out of nothing. And I can tell you, if you're newly married and broke, that God will make a way out of no way.

The motto of my "business" in those days is a proverb I still cling to:

Train up a child

in the way he should go,

And when he is old

he will not depart from it.

—PROVERBS 22:6

Now your child may wander away for a while. He may test the waters in the deep end of the world. She may question and argue and fuss and fume. But he or she will only wander so far before coming back. You can be sure, with every act of kindness, with every word of wisdom, with every loving service you provide for your children, you are leaving a legacy behind.

Our culture has told us by means of marketing that we women need to be controlling this or taking charge of that, fulfilling this "vision" or moving through that "passage." The truth about our role as godly women isn't going to be found in the women's studies section at the library or bookstore. Our manual is the Word of God. Turn off the television and ignore the newest fad on Madison Avenue. Open the guidebook that God has given us—the Holy Bible. It tells us all we need to know.

Without question God directs some women to step out of the home and family circle to assume a role of broader management. The woman who works outside of the home simply needs to be obedient to the Word regarding her responsibilities and needs to put herself under the authority of mature Christians. And whatever she does, it should always be in her family's best interest.

Titus 2:5 admonishes godly women to be "discreet, chaste, homemakers, good, obedient to their own husbands, that the word of God may not be blasphemed." Regardless of our status in life, whether we are career women, single women, single parents, or married women with or without children, each of us has been chosen by God to serve others and to live according to His Word. And each of us has her own way of keeping the home. Some of us do it ourselves. Others hire housekeepers. Any way it is accomplished, the fact is that the home is in order. I believe in women's liberation—the liberation we have in Jesus Christ—because whom the Lord sets free is free indeed.

I also realize that we sometimes feel a lack of freedom, and if we don't keep our eyes fixed on God, we can become complainers and whiners. We gripe about the stresses of the job, the kids, the environment, the commercials on television, our past lives, the abuse we once suffered. But as real as these situations may be, we have been instructed to do all things without grumbling. In fact, after discussing Jesus' humility and servant's heart in Philippians 2, Paul goes on to give us a beautiful set of instructions for all the various kinds of work we do:

> *Therefore, my beloved, as you have always obeyed, not as in my presence only, but now much more in my absence, work out your own salvation with fear and trembling; for it is God who works in you both to will and to do for His good pleasure. Do all things without murmuring and disputing, that you may become blameless and harmless, children of God without fault in the midst of a crooked and perverse generation, among whom you shine as lights in the world.* (Philippians 2:12–15)

During the Season of Growth, particularly when finances are tight or you are in the midst of child rearing, you may feel that this time of your life will never pass. What helped me most during those periods of feeling stuck and uninspired was to maximize the moment—and it really is just a moment. Those babies won't be babies forever, the car pool won't always need your car, and the yearlong cycle of after-school sports will come to a final end. And once those days are over, we never get our children back in quite the same way again. I hope you'll treasure them, and treasure every month of every year you have with them. You'll miss them terribly once they are grown and gone.

I also encourage you to give yourself a break now and then. I always tried to enjoy a mother's day out whenever the opportunity presented itself. Ask friends and family to help you, and do something helpful for them in return. Try to find a Christian day care center where you can occasionally leave the kids for a few hours. Just be careful to choose a safe environment where your children can continue to be encouraged in the faith of their parents.

SERVING OTHERS, SERVING GOD

Esther's service—as we will see in the following chapters—turned out to be extremely dangerous. But she saw a need and she met the need. I am sure she wasn't especially excited about serving in those depressing conditions, not knowing what the end results would be. All she could do was trust in an all-knowing God and accept the wisdom of her uncle Mordecai. Because he had been gracious to her and had taken her in when her parents died, she owed him a debt of gratitude. Mordecai didn't have to take Esther in—he did it because of love and a sense of family service. We read that even after she became queen, Esther did not tell the king about her Jewish nationality because of her loyalty to Mordecai and his instructions to her: "For Esther obeyed the command of Mordecai as when she was brought up by him" (Esther 2:20).

When we think about the Lord's goodness in our lives, when we think about the fact that He didn't have to send His Son to die for us, that Jesus didn't have to come to earth to be sacrificed for us, shouldn't our service be our way of saying thanks? Shouldn't we follow His example out of gratitude and thanksgiving? Service to God is a little bit more significant than busywork, or obligation, or "It's a nasty job but someone has to do it."

Let's try to remember Esther, who knew she had a purpose bigger than herself. Esther was trained in her traditions and she was proud of being Jewish. Do we know who we are? Do we see ourselves as God's chosen people? Do we realize that we are women of influence in the King's royal court? Esther's God was the same God as yours and mine. She knew that He had a plan for her life. Are we as confident in Him as she was?

But maybe you aren't sure what I mean when I use the word *ser-*

vice. Quite simply, whether at home, at school, at work, at church, or in the community, service is what we provide when we see a need that we can meet and then meet it. Service is not limited to things that can be seen, recognized, or applauded publicly. Service is every act of help or mercy we do for the glory of God.

And—please don't forget this—service does *not* mean that we don't take care of ourselves. Sometimes women and men take the idea of service to the extreme and forget their own needs. They overtax their bodies. Their lives are in chaos. They become overwhelmed with feelings of exhaustion and "being used." More often than not, their families are also lacking. This happens when people confuse doing things for God with doing things because they want to impress others or win their approval.

Along similar lines, service has its limitations. Whatever you do, don't let people talk you into serving because they make you feel guilty. True service doesn't include misuse or abuse, although you may feel some discomfort. And if those you serve do not receive your help graciously and in the spirit in which it was given, Luke 9:5 says, "When you go out of that city, shake off the very dust from your feet as a testimony against them."

There are specific principles the Lord requires us to follow as His disciples, and some of them are nonnegotiable. Here's one of them: When the Holy Spirit says, "Go," or "Stay," we are to obey Him. We have to learn to listen, and we have to be willing to do what we're told. God has designed different forms of service for us to accomplish. Sometimes we don't see ourselves as the right person for the job. But that's God's decision, not ours.

I am sure that when Esther was presented as the new queen of Persia, somebody thought she was too young. Somebody else probably said, "She's too inexperienced. She's just not capable." Maybe she herself asked, "How did I end up in the royal palace? I don't belong here!" Whether these things were true or not, the fact remains that when God calls, He also equips. He uses the feeble things of this world to get His work done, for then He gets the greatest glory. Those looking on in amazement shake their heads and say, "It could only be God!"

And let's be real—serving others is sometimes a thankless position. One woman can be mother, wife, employee, nurse, P.T.A. president, decision maker, accountant, chef, counselor, comforter, provider, lover, and teacher. She plays all these many roles in the course of one day and still has a list a mile long for the next day. At the end of the day instead of hearing "Thank you!" she will be asked, "What's for dinner?" or "Are my clothes clean for tomorrow?"

FOR EVERYTHING THERE IS A SEASON

God's gifts to His people are certainly not limited to skills that help us cook and clean and fold clothes. He has also gifted us with spiritual gifts that He intends for us to use in His service to one another. We are to use our gifts, according to Ephesians 4:12–13, "for the equipping of the saints for the work of ministry, for the edifying of the body of Christ, till we all come to the unity of the faith and the knowledge of the Son of God, to a perfect man, to the measure of the stature of the fullness of Christ."

During Esther's time, she was also given unique gifts for use among her people. She was given a prestigious role in the royal household. She was given access to the king. She was given favor in his sight. All those things came from God and were given with the intention of delivering and blessing His people. However, when God's gifts are beneficial to us personally, we may be tempted to use them for our own benefit. Esther faced the challenge of whether she would use her God-given position only for her own comfort or also for the benefit of others. Would she be selfish or a servant?

Because she was well grounded in her traditions and in her calling, Esther found the courage to act with strength and integrity when her time for service came. Although she struggled with the demands brought upon her by the Jewish people's plight, she put her faith in God's providence and found His strength available within her. Because of the faith of her fathers, and the lessons she had learned from Mordecai, she had inner resources to draw upon.

Nonetheless, Esther was afraid of what her service could cost her. And she was wise to wonder—she could have lost her life in the process. It is always risky to serve others and to invest our gifts in God's people. We have to be vulnerable. We have to face the possibility of rejection. We have to risk criticism and failure. But it is only when we step out in faith and invest our gifts in His service that we are able to see the power of God at work and the blessing He has in store for us.

The Word of God tells us that each believer has a special role to play in the function of Christ's body. No one believer can do everything. That's why chapters 12 and 13 of 1 Corinthians speak in the context of love when they tell about spiritual gifts and their use. When the body works together, God's program is propelled forward. The same thing happens in a family. When each family member esteems the gifts of the other, then the family flourishes.

Esther esteemed her people enough to lay her life on the line for them. And she knew she couldn't do it on her own—she prayed and fasted before she stepped into the king's presence. Sometimes the requests and obligations we have to deal with drive us to our knees, which is the best possible place to begin our work. Fasting and prayer remind us how much we need God's help, and they remind us of His power. Even though fasting drains and saps our physical strength, in our weakness He is made strong. His power produces success. His help is indispensable—we can't do it without Him.

If we serve in our own strength we become frustrated like Martha, not peaceful like Mary. Mary also served, but she knew when it was time to be refueled. Luke 10:40 says, "My sister has left me to serve alone." The fact that Mary left is key. She was in the kitchen for a while, but then made the choice to balance her priorities of service and relationship with the Master.

Once a session of service to God is over, we all need time to ourselves, to find rest and recreation and retreat. God rested after He finished creating the world; Jesus always took Himself away to spend time alone with the Father. Should we do any less? Times of rest give us strength to carry on until the task is complete, until the service is accomplished, until the season has passed.

Stop for a moment. Like Mary, listen carefully. Can you hear the voice of Jesus calling to you even now?

"Come to Me,
all you who labor and are heavy laden,

and I will give you rest.
Take My yoke upon you and learn from Me,
for I am gentle and lowly in heart,
and you will find rest for your souls.
For My yoke is easy and My burden is light."
—MATTHEW 11:28–30

Preparation

Each young woman's turn came to go in to King Ahasuerus
after she had completed twelve months' preparation,
according to the regulations for the women,
for thus were the days of their preparation apportioned:
six months with oil of myrrh,
and six months with perfumes and preparations for beautifying women.
Thus prepared, each young woman went to the king,
and she was given whatever she desired to take with her
from the women's quarters to the king's palace.
—ESTHER 2:12–13

Do you feel that life is standing still? Does it seem that day after day nothing changes and that God has forgotten you? No, He hasn't forgotten. He is simply taking the time to prepare you for a special task, for a future opportunity. Preparation, along with obedience and service, is part of God's process in the Season of Growth. Like Esther, we have to be prepared for our King, to be of help to His people.

Because we don't always understand God's ways, at times we may think we are ready for anything. We've been reading the Word. We've been in prayer. We've been listening to good teaching. What else do we have to do?

Esther could have said, "I don't need all this preparation! The king saw me and fell in love with me at first sight. Isn't that the point?" In a similar sense, we might say, "Jesus died so I could have free salvation and all the benefits of being a coheir. Isn't that enough? Why do I have to go through any process of preparation?"

It's true. Jesus saw us in our pitiful enslavement to sin, and in spite of everything, He fell head over heels in love with us. His love gave us free salvation and saved us from a future separation from Him. But in order for heaven to come down to us in our day-to-day realities, we have to prepare. Our position in Christ is secure, but our journey here on earth has directions that need to be followed if we want to have a fruitful life. Philippians 2:12 (NIV) says, "Work out your salvation with fear and trembling." There are necessary times of preparation in our lives. Like Esther, we need to pass through times of cleansing, times of purifying, and times of anointing.

When we begin our walk with Jesus, His blood cleanses from all sin, and because of His holiness, we are declared holy too. But there are stains on our characters that can lead us back into sin and failure. God has to do a work of cleaning to remove our flaws. *This process is called sanctification, and it goes on throughout our lives.* In the Season of Growth, an intense time of cleansing is necessary before we fully enter into the future He has planned for us.

The purification of our thoughts and motives is part of this process of cleansing. Because we live in the world system, we have learned certain patterns of thinking and acting that may not be in accordance with His will. God wants to transform our thought life, so that the motives that lie behind our actions will be pure and godly. He wants to make sure that the meditations of our hearts are pleasing in His sight (Psalm 19:14).

And God wants to anoint us for life in His kingdom. Esther was bathed in rich, fragrant oil. We need to utilize the anointing of the Holy Spirit so God can send us out into the world, ready and able to use the spiritual gifts He has given us. His desire is that our prayers and good works will drift into His presence like sweet-smelling incense.

All of this takes time, and we have to believe that God knows what He is doing while we go through the preparation process. Esther's confidence grew during the time she spent in preparation. She would have felt far more afraid going into the king's presence if she hadn't passed through the process of royal preparation.

Esther moved around during those months, but she had to stay within the palace walls. Although it may have been restricting and confining, my girl was still in the palace! Your Christian life might seem confining and restrictive, too. However, it's important to remember that you are also in a palace being taken care of by the King of Kings. Palaces are big places, and there's a lot to see, so make the best use of your time.

Now Esther could have decided when it was the best time to see the king. She could have manipulated and maneuvered her way into his presence. Some of us choose to come up with our own plans, but then we have to live with the consequences. Yes, we need to be active Christians, walking through doors that are open to us. But sometimes we break the doors down, say they were already open, and even use God's name to defend ourselves, defiling His character with misinterpretations of His Word. We do these things to meet our own needs instead of trusting Him.

While God prepares you, and it seems that time is standing still, it's helpful to remember whose we are and where we are. It is better to be standing still in His will than moving around at high speed outside of it. I once heard a woman say that she would rather be in a mud hut in a Third World country in God's will than in a mansion in North America, if that mansion lay outside of His will.

"But you don't understand," you may be saying. "This has been going on way too long. If I had to wait one year I could handle it, but I have been waiting five, ten, twenty years!"

God's timing is a mystery. If we start comparing the time we spend waiting with the time *others* spend, we will be terribly frustrated. God has a unique design for each of our lives. And because He is a God of variety, our time of preparation and our Season of Growth will be unlike that of anyone else.

Look at it this way: If you are making a king-size quilt, it could take several years to finish it. If you are making a baby quilt, you will probably finish that in a year or less. It all depends on what the quilt-maker is designing. How complicated is the pattern? How small are the pieces? How intricate is the stitching? The Bible says that we are God's handiwork. That helps explain the amount of time He spends working on each of our lives.

PREPARATION — A LADY-IN-WAITING

Esther's goal was to go before the king, to be welcomed and not rejected, and to ask him to be merciful to the Jews. Our goals are different, but like her, it will take time for us to achieve them satisfactorily. We may need more education. We may need to get in better physical shape. We may require spiritual growth and insight. We may need to mature emotionally. Whatever it is we need to do, some of it will be done with the help of others, but most of it will be done in private.

I know that solitude is not our favorite pastime. Neither is waiting. We want to skip this whole stage because it is time-consuming and we're anxious to get on with business. Maybe we should always ask ourselves a couple of questions. *Whose business is it we want to get on with? And whose schedule are we on?* If you are on God's schedule, you can rest in the knowledge that He is in control, His timing is perfect, and He doesn't make mistakes.

Making the decision to stay at home with my kids until they went to school was tough, and as I said before, those days seemed endless at the time. For years I was invited to speak, and when I gave my best shot at saying no, some people responded in horror. "You don't take speaking engagements? But how can that be? You're a pastor's wife. You are Tony Evans's wife. You have to be able to speak!"

I would respond as kindly as possible, "You're right on all counts. But you see, I'm waiting for my release papers from my Designer. As soon as He gives me the OK, I'll be happy to speak."

Now I wasn't idle during my time of waiting. I prepared, I studied, I attended many conferences and seminars. I gathered materials that ministered to me, and I finished my degree. I used all the resources and opportunities that were afforded me during that time. And as soon as the Lord released me with His peace, I started speaking publicly.

During the preparation time, you can fuss and fight or you can rest in the reality that He knows what is best and will not withhold any good thing from you. The closer you get to the Lord, the more confidence you will develop in Him. You will come to see that if He could lead His people across the Red Sea, if He could feed five thousand with two fish and five barley loaves, then certainly He can meet your needs and mine.

Does this time of waiting, this period of preparation, this Season of Growth loom over you like a huge mountain? I love what Bill Hybels says in his book *Too Busy Not to Pray: Slowing Down to Be with God* (Downers Grove, Ill.: 1988, 70–71):

> How do you pray a prayer so filled with faith that it can move a mountain? By shifting the focus from the size of your mountain to the sufficiency of the mountain mover, and by stepping forward in obedience. . . .
>
> While the children of Israel are perched on the edge of the Promised Land, twelve spies go out to survey it. Ten came back saying, "You wouldn't believe the size of the cities, the armies, the giants. We'd better look somewhere else." Two come back saying, "The God who is faithful promised he would give us the land, so let's go in his strength." Ten looked at the size of the mountain and fell back: only two looked at the sufficiency of the mountain mover and wanted to move forward. (Read the story in Numbers 13.) . . .
>
> I challenge you to shift the focus of your prayer. Don't spend a lot of your time describing your mountain to the Lord. He knows what it is. Instead, focus your attention on the mountain mover— his glory, power, and faithfulness. Then start walking in faith, following his leading, and watch that mountain step aside.

PREPARATION FOR THE WORST

Of course God prepares us for the good works He has planned for us. He gets us ready for mountaintops of ministry, for peaks of productivity. But He is also a master at preparing us to handle valleys, even when we don't see them coming, even when we don't know what He's doing at the time.

One day I had just dropped off the children to school and was on my way to work. Suddenly I developed an acute sense of nervousness and was incapable of driving. I pulled over to the side of the road and prayed for help. And God started ministering to me. Scripture after Scripture ripped through my soul—Romans 8:28; 1 Corinthians 10:31; Psalm 23; Philippians 4:19, and a number of others. After a while I was able to regroup and carry on. However, I knew deep in my heart that the Lord was preparing me for something.

Two weeks later Chrystal called from college. She was crying so intensely that she couldn't keep her composure. She couldn't even talk. Finally, she was able to pull herself together well enough to speak. And I was able to hear those dreadful words, "Mommy, I'm pregnant."

After the initial shock, Tony and I found strength in the Lord. We immediately started mapping out a plan of action related to finishing college and delivering a baby. But two weeks later I crumbled under the load of disappointment. I kept asking God, "Why? Why would You let this happen?"

My remorse and sorrow were for His Name's sake. Tony and I would carry on, maybe not in the pastorate we thought, but we would carry on for our daughter's sake, for our family's sake. Our major sadness was based on the fact that Tony was pastoring a large flock and we had disappointed them.

My cry of "Why, God, why?" wasn't voiced out of anger. It was a human cry, a mother's cry, a cry of desperation out of my own agony. If the Lord Jesus cried out from His cross, "My God, My God, why have You forsaken Me?", I think it is OK for us to ask the "Why" questions too. Over the years I've discovered it's no sin to ask the Lord why things happen. God can handle our questions. But here's the important thing: Can we handle His answers?

Why does God allow hurt to come into our lives? Again, we can relate to Esther. Certainly she had to deal with some difficult questions of her own. Why did she lose her parents? Why were the Jews enslaved by the Persians? Why was she in the king's court when so many Jewish girls were suffering outside the palace walls? First Peter 4:12–13 (NIV) says, "Dear friends, do not be surprised at the painful trial you are suffering, as though something strange were happening to you. But rejoice that you participate in the sufferings of Christ, so that you may be overjoyed when his glory is revealed."

During those challenging days when we came to terms with Chrystal's pregnancy, the Lord ministered grace to us through the church. He demonstrated to us that He is a God of love. And by love, I mean that He does what is best for us. Do you wonder what could be best for us in that situation? So did we at the time. Only the Lord knows what He is trying to accomplish in and through us, even when negative things come into our lives. For us, He showed His greatness in the fact that we lacked nothing.

For several months before Chrystal's call, Tony and I had discussed a longing in our hearts for another child. We had come to the conclusion that our only option was to adopt. I remember making the statement, "I will only adopt a child from within the family or from a close family friend. I don't want to adopt a child from a total stranger."

God works in His own ways. The birth of Kariss, our granddaughter, met the deepest need in the life of our family.

And what about the pregnancy itself? How should we respond when our children make mistakes? Isaiah 53:6 (NIV) says, "We all, like sheep, have gone astray, each of us has turned to his own way." God, the perfect Father, the best possible Parent, has children who stray. Even His perfect parenting does not prevent it. Our heavenly Father has to endure the choices of His children that violate His principles. We are in good company when our children go wrong. God understands our grief. The next time your children's failures make you feel like you've done it all wrong, deal honestly with your own failures. But also remember—you can lead a child to the waters of wisdom, but you cannot make him drink. Let's just hope and pray that our investment in our children's lives will cause them to thirst for the Living Water, which can only be found in Jesus.

A SEASON FOR EVERYTHING

What is God preparing you for? You might have some indications about the future as you move through your seasons. It could be a gradual revelation, where little by little you see growth. It could be a complete mystery, in which you have no choice but to walk by faith. At an early age I was exposed to both music and business. Not only did I enjoy them, but also I realized that I had natural ability and that every door I knocked on in those fields opened up for me. Once I stepped through and excelled, I asked myself, *Could this be what God has called me to?* I wasn't absolutely sure, but I put my hand to the plow and forged ahead.

At times, it really was a *forging* ahead, because I kept running into wonderful people who had already determined what God wanted me to do, especially as a pastor's wife. It must be directing the choir, it must be heading up the children's ministry, it must be leading the ladies' ministry, it must be counseling, it must be, it must be. Although all those things have their rightful place, and I have played a role in all of them to some degree, as it turned out, my specific call and gifts were not fulfilled in any of those areas.

At times like that, when the clamor around you is drowning out God's still, small voice, you need a Mordecai. You need someone in your life who will encourage you to follow the course the Master has laid out, to run the race with endurance. Listen to your mentors and remember the proverb attributed to the Chinese philosopher Lao-tzu: "A journey of a thousand miles must begin with a single step." Take one step at a time and only step where He leads.

As you abide in Him, you will naturally begin to think His thoughts. It is possible to be so close to Him that your thought life reflects His desires and direction for your life. Have you ever been around people who have been married so long that they even get to the point where they act like each other and say the same thing at the same time? Sometimes they even look alike.

That is exactly how close to the Savior we want to be, so that our thoughts are His thoughts and His way is ours. He wants us to look like Him. People should see us coming and say, "There goes a disciple of Jesus Christ. She acts just like Him." John 15:7 promises, "If you abide in Me, and My words abide in you, you will ask what you desire, and it shall be done for you." What an open-ended statement! Ask whatever you wish and it shall be done. I want to know Him like that, don't you? But you can be sure that it will take lots of preparation time. It takes time to learn to abide.

Now you have some choices. You can be like some tea drinkers. You can let the bag stay in the hot water, or you can dip it in and out of the cup because you do not want it to get too strong. If you want to have a full life in Christ, saturate yourself in His Word and steep yourself in prayer. He will probably take you through some hot water to make you strong, but you will be strong indeed.

Although, throughout our lives, we are always called to obey, to serve, and to be prepared for whatever God has for us, the rigorous Season of Growth doesn't last forever. This too will pass. Ecclesiastes 3:1–13 tells us that there is a time for everything, and after this Season of Growth, we will enter a new season, the Season of Harvest. Meanwhile, that beautiful section of God's Word ends with some encouraging words for those of us who obey, serve, and wait while He prepares us for the future.

> *He has made everything beautiful in its time.*
> *Also He has put eternity in their hearts,*
> *except that no man can find out*
> *the work that God does from beginning to end.*
> *I know that there is nothing better for them than to rejoice,*
> *and to do good in their lives,*
> *and also that every man should eat and drink*
> *and enjoy the good of all his labor—it is the gift of God.*
> —ECCLESIASTES 3:11–13

PART

THREE

The
Season
of
Harvest

CHAPTER
SEVEN

Contentment, Not Complacency

[Mordecai] also gave [Hathach] a copy of the written decree
for their destruction, which was given at Shushan,
that he might show it to Esther and explain it to her,
and that he might command her to go in to the king
to make supplication to him and plead before him for her people.
So Hathach returned and told Esther the words of Mordecai.
Then Esther spoke to Hathach, and gave him a command for Mordecai:
"All the king's servants and the people of the king's provinces
know that any man or woman who goes into the inner court to the king,
who has not been called, he has but one law:
put all to death, except the one to whom the king
holds out the golden scepter, that he may live.
Yet I myself have not been called to go in to the king these thirty days."
So they told Mordecai Esther's words.
Then Mordecai told them to answer Esther:
"Do not think in your heart that you will escape in the king's palace
any more than all the other Jews."

—ESTHER 4:8–13

The word *contentment* describes a feeling of satisfaction; it means
we are happy enough with what we have or with what we are do-

ing. Contentment implies that we don't desire something more or crave something different. First Timothy 6:6–8 says, "Godliness with contentment is great gain. For we brought nothing into this world, and it is certain we can carry nothing out. And having food and clothing, with these we shall be content."

Contentment is a good thing, a godly thing. But at times our contentment can lull us into a different experience—complacency. Complacency is a state of self-satisfaction or smugness. It takes our eyes off the Lord and His plans and fixes them on ourselves and our comfort zone. Complacency can take us away from the source of our blessing. We can fall so in love with our surroundings that we lose sight of our call.

Complacency causes us to become lazy in our current situation, and therefore we miss out on the future blessings God has prepared for us. First Timothy 6:6–8 says that if we have the basic needs of life met we should be content. An "attitude of gratitude" honors what God has already done for us. Contentment *does not* mean "I do not wish to better my lot in life." That's complacency. It *does* mean that I am going to enjoy what I have and be grateful for it while I'm waiting and working for my lot to change.

Esther became very comfortable and content in the palace, even to the point of losing her focus, of remembering why she was placed in a royal role to begin with. She nearly allowed her circumstances, power, and money to obscure her divine perspective. She came very close to moving from contentment to complacency.

When we look at things from a heavenly perspective, we view life differently and remember that all good things come from above. We keep in mind the fact that without the Lord, we can do nothing. No matter what is going on in your life, contentment means you have an inner peace, knowing that God is going through the season with you. Contentment is realizing that after you have done all you can, you can rest in the awareness that God can complete His good work in your life without your help.

When you are able to find contentment in whatever season you are in, enjoy the blessing. It might be a stage in your life where you do not have a lot of this world's toys, but you still have peace. Philippians 4:9 says, "The things which you learned and received and heard and saw in me, these do, and the God of peace will be with you." God will always be present in your daily experience when you realize that you can cast all your cares upon Him because He cares for you (see 1 Peter 5:7). He will provide contentment, but it is up to us to receive it.

Contentment comes when you know your heavenly Father—your "Daddy"—not just as an acquaintance, but in an intimate, ongoing relationship. He is not only your Savior, but He is your Good Shepherd. Your Savior will get you to heaven, but your Shepherd will give you the guidance and direction you need on earth.

So often we aren't content because we have been sold the lie that our contentment is based on what we possess. There is nothing wrong with having things, but advertisers constantly remind us of the additional things we could, should, or would have as our own. "If only . . ." Madison Avenue is trying to convince us that by this season of life we should possess all sorts of material goods—and we will be unhappy until we get them. If we listen to their appeals, we find ourselves living in a state of "If only," which keeps us from enjoying the good things God has given us. Our minds become distracted and centered upon the elusive things we don't have.

Like children who are dissatisfied with childhood because they are too concerned with being grown-ups, we sometimes lose our contentment when we become obsessed with the future instead of the present. Remember, we were only promised one day at a time: "Give us *this day* our daily bread" (Matthew 6:11; Luke 11:3, italics added). Matthew 6:33–34 says, "Seek first the kingdom of God and His righteousness, and all these things shall be added to you. Therefore do not worry about tomorrow, for tomorrow will worry about its own things. Sufficient for the day is its own trouble."

During our seminary years, when all Tony and I could feast on was ground beef, I developed several ways to cook what we affectionately called "seminary steak." The recipes I learned from our ground beef days came in handy for the chicken age. They stretched my creativity and gave Tony something to look forward to when he came home from school. We did the best we could with the "manna" the Lord provided for us at that time.

Did we get tired of the seminary steak? Of course we did. But because we could look forward to the future, I produced innumerable sloppy joes, tons of meat loaf, and countless hamburgers, casseroles, and meatballs. I even fried the stuff, when Tony needed a taste of fried food. Every time we had the chance to eat other meat, we took the opportunity and enjoyed it. Finally, as God opened doors for us to move to the next level, we moved on. For us, the "seminary steak" period was a time of contentment but not of complacency.

LEARNING TO BE CONTENT

The more challenging our circumstances, the more difficult it is for us to be content. The children of Israel were restless during their hard trek across the wilderness, and their lack of contentment caused them to fall into sin. They complained that God was unfair to them; they "murmured" against the Lord, telling each other that He had forgotten them (Numbers 14:1–3, 29; cf. 16:41; Deuteronomy 1:27). They created their own false god instead of worshiping the true God, who had already shown them His wonder-working power again and again. Lack of contentment can lead us into carnality.

I was talking with a single parent the other day about all the demands she has to deal with in her life. She has a challenging job in an investment company, working for a highly competitive boss. He is a difficult man because of the company's demanding environment and, as far as he is concerned, *everything* is top priority. I probably don't have to tell you that he also has a very short fuse.

This woman is not only working full-time, but she is studying to be certified as a financial advisor. And, as if that weren't enough, she faces the daily demands of a child with homework and school projects and extracurricular activities. This woman is committed to excellence, but she is nearly overwhelmed by her many responsibilities.

Her question to me was fairly straightforward: "What should I do? I can't meet the demands, yet I have to work; I have to provide. Is there another way?"

"There are several other ways," I told her. "Let's take a look at them. First of all, could you live with less money? Could you find another job that pays less, requires less of you, and still gives you the benefits you now receive? Another question: Is there any other profession you would like to do until your child is older? Maybe you could substitute teach, so you could be with your child."

There was a moment of silence on the line. Then the woman said, "Um, no. None of that sounds especially appealing."

"OK," I continued, "then maybe the Lord wants to stretch you for a reason that we can't see right now. Because it sounds like you need the income and benefits that this job offers."

I went on to suggest that she evaluate all the extracurricular activities, to see which of them could be done in some other year, during the summer, or cut out completely. I finally said, "This season in your life seems to be work and more work, school and more school. I know it is sometimes unbearable, but God knows what He is doing, and maybe there are lessons to be learned."

Then she explained that her desire was to work for a certain number of years, then take an extended vacation to Europe, buy a home, and open up her own financial investment firm. Well, I recommended that she take down the posters of Europe from her walls and hang up a Scripture: "Trust in the Lord with all your heart, and lean not on your own understanding; in all your ways acknowledge Him, and He shall direct your paths" (Proverbs 3:5–6).

I knew that if this woman continued to long for some future fantasy, if she persisted in fixing her eyes on the problems of today, she would crash and burn. It was important for her to look up, to turn her eyes upon Jesus, to trust Him with the present, and to rely on Him to provide her with a future that would bless her and her son.

"Let Him tell you His plans; you don't need to tell Him yours," I advised her. We prayed together. A few days later, I received a call saying that even in her despair, this hardworking woman had found a sense of peace. She still had her dreams, but they weren't standing in the way of her present satisfaction. She had discovered contentment.

Now don't get me wrong. There's nothing wrong with dreaming. Dreams are essential to our lives. If, in the early days, Tony and I had looked at our present reality to determine the future, it would have painted a bleak picture. We would have been miserable people, feeling deprived and consumed with nothing but exhausting priorities and ceaseless responsibilities. But I was fortunate. Not only did I have the Lord, but I had Tony in my life. He was a light in a dark tunnel. He has always dreamed, and he has taught me to dream, too, and to have hope for the future.

Nowadays, we look back and marvel at what God's grace has done, and we are thankful as we continue to look to the future for even more of His grace. In every season of our lives, where there is life there is always hope, no matter what the challenges. When God is in our dreams, our dreams can't help but come true. Meanwhile, take it from me. It pays to hang around people who encourage you to be thankful in the present even as you look to the future He has prepared.

A ROYAL WAKE-UP CALL

We have to find a balance in our lives. Sometimes we have to find contentment in difficult circumstances. And sometimes we have to be careful that our comfortable surroundings don't keep us from getting up, moving forward, and fulfilling God's plan for us.

When we reflect upon Esther's time of preparation, it was for the most part a lovely experience. She was pampered, beautified, and kept from any sort of unnecessary stress. Other than the inevitable jealous squabbles that probably broke out in the king's harem, Esther had few problems. She was surrounded by luxury, fed the finest foods, and clothed in the most beautiful garments. She lacked nothing and had little to fear.

Then she heard the news about Mordecai. For some reason he was fasting, was ripping his clothes, was acting like a desperate man. When she inquired about his behavior, she was told about Haman's terrible plot against the Jewish people. And Mordecai had a specific message for Esther: *"Do not think in your heart that you will escape in the king's palace any more than all the other Jews"* (Esther 4:13).

"Don't kid yourself, Esther," Mordecai was saying. "You may be living in the lap of luxury today, but once this edict to kill all the Jews is acted upon, your heritage will be found out. You'll be murdered along with the rest of us."

Little by little, Esther must have forgotten that she was in a unique situation. Days of preferential treatment had caused her to put out of her mind the miracle that she had ever found her way into the palace to begin with. She had grown used to the idea that she was the king's favorite. She was a rising star. Maybe she'd even imagined that she had done it all on her own.

But now a cold tide of reality swept away the last traces of her fantasy. Her sense of complacency was shattered. She could no longer remain in a place of blissful delight. Mordecai wouldn't let her. Her heart wouldn't let her. And God had a better idea.

What do you do when there is no way out of a situation? You have plotted and planned and still you're stuck. Like the decision some make to stay home with their children, what keeps you there, even when the walls are closing in? Sometimes it is only commitment, and nothing else. We simply decide to be content with the commitment we have made, and let the chips fall where they may.

Contentment involves sacrifice. Esther had to take a risk, and that risk might well have cost her her life. No matter what our commitment may be, sometimes we feel that way. Esther learned, and so must we, that God will never lead us where He will not keep us. Danger and difficulty simply produce in us a better perspective of His power and His peace. Let's learn to trust God's heart when we can't see His hand.

The prophet Habakkuk said, in the midst of his struggle, "Yet I will rejoice in the Lord, I will joy in the God of my salvation. The Lord God is my strength; He will make my feet like deer's feet, and He will make me walk on my high hills" (Habakkuk 3:18–19). Deer's feet may be rough and callused, but they can step with surefootedness without slipping. Habakkuk's faith and confidence in the Lord helped him to endure a barren season. As God's women in a slippery world, with the Lord's help, we too need to develop surefootedness. We need to be women who hold onto Christ; we need Him to order our steps in the Word (Psalm 37:23–24).

Our commitments will stretch us. Sometimes they stretch us so far that our fig tree dries up. That's when we need to take inventory of what God has done for us in the past. We need to ask Him to give us our joy back as we worship Him. Tough commitments require us to develop a life of praise and worship. When praise becomes a habit, it is our lifeline. It is like a cable. We weave a thread of it each day, and soon it becomes so strong we cannot break it.

Oliver Wendell Holmes wrote, "I find the great thing in this world is not so much where we stand, as in what direction we are moving." Because Esther was uncertain about the response of the king to her attempt to save the Jews, she had to go into God's presence with fasting and prayer. She needed the strength not to be complacent, just sitting back and enjoying the status quo. Complacency means doing nothing; contentment does not. Contentment means that when you have done all that is within your power, you trust God with everything else.

Contentment can exist no matter what circumstance we are in. Paul writes that he was content whether he abounded or was abased, whether he had a little or a lot (Philippians 4:12). He made these statements when he was in a similar situation to Esther's, not knowing whether he would live or die (Philippians 1:21–24). God was so real to him on the inside that he could handle anything on the outside.

Grace should produce gratitude, and gratitude should evoke service. If we really appreciate the grace of God, then we will seek opportunities to do things for Him. God had graciously given Esther a high opportunity. She had become comfortable. She had grown content. Would she prove herself complacent to the plight of her people? Like Esther, we face the temptation to be selfish and only think of our personal peace and affluence. It is wrong for us to take and receive from God's goodness without demonstrating our thanksgiving in service to others.

One of the principles of Christianity is that "unless a grain of wheat falls into the ground and dies," it can bear no fruit (John 12:24). As Christians, we cannot enter into the Season of Harvest unless we lay our lives down. Fortunately, Esther remembered the goodness God had shown to her. She made the commitment to leverage her position of grace for the benefit of God's chosen people. She put her life on the line. Should we do less?

Therefore we also, since we are surrounded
by so great a cloud of witnesses,
let us lay aside every weight, and the sin which so easily ensnares us,

and let us run with endurance the race that is set before us,
looking unto Jesus, the author and finisher of our faith,
who for the joy that was set before Him endured the cross,
despising the shame,
and has sat down at the right hand of the throne of God.

—HEBREWS 12:1–2

CHAPTER EIGHT

For Such a Time As This

"If you remain completely silent at this time,
relief and deliverance will arise for the Jews from another place,
but you and your father's house will perish.
Yet who knows whether you have come to the kingdom
for such a time as this?"
Then Esther told them to return this answer to Mordecai:
"Go, gather all the Jews who are present in Shushan, and fast for me;
neither eat nor drink for three days, night or day.
My maids and I will fast likewise.
And so I will go to the king, which is against the law;
and if I perish, I perish!"
—ESTHER 4:14–16

Esther, the beautiful queen of Persia, suddenly found herself faced with a very big problem. The wicked Haman had not only plotted to kill all the Jews throughout the country—including Queen Esther, if Haman had known she was Jewish—but he had already sent out the "death sentence" edict to all the provinces of the country. Once her uncle Mordecai explained the dismal situation to her, Esther finally realized that she would have to intervene by going to see the king.

There was a rule in the palace that if the queen walked into the king's presence without being invited, he could interpret that as a sign of disrespect and she would be immediately killed. Considering that the king's last wife had proved herself very disrespectful to him, we can only assume that the king was especially sensitive to that kind of behavior. On the other hand, if Esther didn't somehow find the courage to step into the king's presence, she and all the other Jewish people would lose their lives.

Needless to say, Esther was scared. Wouldn't you be?

Fear is a valid emotion. We need fear to warn us of danger, to alert us when things aren't quite right. But fear is not valid when it begins to control us. Our minds need to set the course of our lives, not our emotions. And fear is a very unpredictable emotion. It can manifest itself in many ways and, if left unattended, can rob us of joy, immobilize us in our homes, and destroy our lives.

Fear can be destructive to both inner and outer beauty. It can produce tension, which keeps us uptight and irritable. It can create mistrust, until we are always questioning the motives of everything and everyone. Fear begets unhappiness because it causes us to focus on negatives, always looking to see what is going to go wrong next. Fear instigates nervous reactions to everything. When we are afraid, a genuine smile can become the most difficult exercise. Instead, our faces are lined and our brows furrowed. Fear even changes the way we walk and move our bodies.

Fear can often be satanic, and just like the deceiver himself, it can come at you in different forms and disguises. Have you ever struggled with fear? It can attack you in your home. You start to think, *Is my husband having an affair? Are my kids on drugs? Do I have cancer? Am I a liability to my husband's life and ministry? Would he be better off without me?*

Fear can be a hindrance at work. *Will I ever get promoted? Do my coworkers hate me? Does the boss know how hard I work? Did I put everything in the children's lunch kits? Do my kids and my husband appreciate everything I do for them?*

Fear can cause us all kinds of trouble at church. *Do I look as good as those women over there? Did I leave the stove on? I wish I hadn't confided in the pastor—I'm afraid he'll preach about my situation.*

That girl over there surely doesn't look much like a Christian. Do I look as worldly as she does? Am I singing on key?

Fear can be a problem on a very personal level. *Will anyone ever really love me? Is something wrong with me—something everyone sees but me? Will I ever get married? Will I ever have children? Will I die young? Am I too fat? Too skinny? Too old? Too young? Too uneducated? Too smart for my own good?*

The devil's game is to distract us from the things of the Lord. And the Lord has told us that fear doesn't come from Him. Paul wrote, "God has not given us a spirit of fear, but of power and of love and of a sound mind" (2 Timothy 1:7). And John reminds us, "There is no fear in love; but perfect love casts out fear, because fear involves torment. But he who fears has not been made perfect in love" (1 John 4:18).

There is only one form of fear that is healthy for us. The Bible tells us that "the fear of the Lord is the beginning of wisdom" (Psalm 111:10; Proverbs 9:10; cf. Job 28:28; Proverbs 1:7). But this is a different kind of fear altogether. To fear God means to reverence Him, to hold Him in awe. That kind of godly fear leads to obedience, because we realize His power as well as His love for us.

"That's fine, Lois," you may be saying. "But I have a huge problem with fear. What are some practical steps I can take in order to overcome it?"

First, we can make up our minds to fight our fears with the Word of God, which is the sword of the Spirit (Ephesians 6:17). This is a matter of the will. Fear often happens because of our lack of faith in God and our ignorance about His Word. The Lord has given us the capacity to overcome our fears by memorizing Scripture and quoting it when we are afraid.

Second, we can walk in the Spirit, not in the flesh. We have to realize that fear comes not only from the devil; it also rises from the flesh. We need to heed the Bible, which says, "Walk in the Spirit, and you shall not fulfill the lust of the flesh. For the flesh lusts against the Spirit, and the Spirit against the flesh; and these are contrary to one another, so that you do not do the things that you wish" (Galatians 5:16–17).

Third, we can claim victory over fear every minute of the day.

Every time you feel a twinge of fear, claim His promise: "I will never leave you nor forsake you" (Hebrews 13:5). Remember R.P.T? *Rejoice, Praise, Trust for Resurrection Power Today.* It really works. I want you to know that the Lord has helped me and is still helping me deal with fear in my own life. And I can't express how much more comfortable my life is when I relax in Him. I know He'll take care of you in the same way He takes care of me.

I have also learned that there is an equation in all this:

Fear activates the devil
Faith activates the Lord

Little faith will bring your soul to heaven; great faith will bring heaven to your soul. Faith will produce victorious Christian living. Faith will overcome our fear. Faith will defeat our enemy, Satan. Esther turned to faith and to the people of God to help her overcome her fear—a fear that warned of very real danger.

FEAR OF FLYING

After reading about my "little plane, little faith" dilemma, you have probably figured out by now that flying is not one of my favorite things to do. In the past, a week before my trips I would find myself becoming indecisive and nervous. I knew in my head that the Lord would take care of me, but my emotions sometimes took over the controls. Over the years, I have given this area of my life to the Lord, and He has brought me to the point where what I know about Him is becoming more and more part of my reality.

Fear comes when there is a lack of *faith* in God and His Word, not a lack of *knowledge.* If we could only get around to using the Word we know, we would have more victories in our Christian walk. More and more, I have learned that the time I take to dwell on the negative should instead be time I spend meditating on His promises. When we use the Word, Satan has to flee. In Matthew 4:10 Jesus used the Word to tell the devil, "Away with you, Satan!" We have to recognize that fear comes from Satan and refuse to let him control us.

The Christian walk is a moment-by-moment walk, and we have to decide every moment to whom we will yield our emotions. The

Lord promises that if we call on Him, He is there to answer us. Hebrews 13:5 says, "[God] Himself has said, 'I will never leave you nor forsake you.'" The Scripture says *never*, so in those times of despair, who has moved? He has not, so it behooves us to draw near to Him.

Psalm 34:4 affirms, "I sought the Lord, and He heard me, and delivered me from all my fears." Focusing on the sovereign nature and perfect purposes of our eternal God allows us to regain control in our lives, finding godly wisdom and confidence in every situation. He has helped me and is still helping me in this difficult area of flying. And when I place my confidence in Him, I cannot express how much more relaxed and comfortable my life is. Here are three important points that have helped me:

- The Lord has given us the capacity to overcome fear (Romans 8:15).
- Our enemy is Satan, and we must refuse to let him control us (Galatians 5:16).
- We have to decide to whom we will yield ourselves (1 John 4:4).

PRAYING AND FASTING FOR THE KINGDOM'S SAKE

In all his satanic hatred, Haman thought he had everything arranged to trap and destroy Mordecai. But if Esther could gain control over her fear, she would be able to approach the king and share with him her needs and the needs of her people. How could Esther come to that point? How did she find the confidence she needed to do God's will?

Esther did not see the hand of God supernaturally begin to work in her life until she and her fellow believers entered into God's presence through fasting and prayer. Fasting means giving up a craving of the flesh because we have a greater need of the spirit. When we fast, we intensify our prayers, instilling them with more power. We sacrifice the physical to gain spiritual power; we do this to overcome the circumstances and burdens in our lives.

It's important to notice that Esther did not try to do all the praying herself. The life of faith is not intended to be lived alone. We need to reach out to one another; we need to support one another with intercessory prayer; we need to bear one another's burdens in prayers of petition. When you get to a point where you just want out, when you don't feel that you have what it takes to accomplish your mission, call on as many godly people as possible to fast and pray. Once you do that, expect to see His power unleashed and His will accomplished in your circumstances.

When I committed my life to Christ to serve Him at the age of fifteen, I had no knowledge of His plan for me. I just knew I was committed to do whatever it was He wanted. Through a series of supernatural events God brought Tony and me together. I was already cultivating my gifts. How could I know that He would use those gifts and skills in ministry on a national level? Yet today God is allowing millions of people to be touched by our ministry on a daily basis.

Romans 12:1–2 talks about the transformation God does within us, working from the inside out. He promises ultimate fulfillment to those who are willing to give their all to God. When we do this, Paul says, we will "prove," or experience, God's will. And His will will amount to the best thing for us, the "acceptable" (we will love the end results) and the "perfect" (complete, without lack).

The question we face as women is a very big one: Are we willing to entrust ourselves to God at that level? Like Esther, we each face the choice of staying in our comfort zone or of taking the risk of obedience.

Even after we have said yes, we should never lose sight of the fact that the Enemy is at work. All through history we can trace Satan's desire to destroy the people of God. And he's just as busy at it today as he was in Esther's time. If you are faced with a situation in which you are being called by God to step out in obedience, you can be sure that you will encounter some opposition along the way.

Satan is going to do everything in his power to stop us in our tracks. Haman, who was acting on Satan's behalf, tried every trick in the book to get rid of God's man and God's people. Instead, he was strung up on the very same gallows he had prepared for Mordecai. In an exquisite exchange of roles, Mordecai then took Haman's place in the palace. God takes good care of His own. It's up to us to pray and fast, trust and obey, while He does His work.

THE COURAGE TO SAY YES

Are you facing some agonizing decisions? Are you determined to obey Him? Saying yes to His will could cost you dearly. Saying yes could mean giving up the completion of your education. It could mean breaking up with a man who is not God's best for you. It could mean delays in reaching that financial peak. It could mean telling the truth when the truth will hurt. Before the fact, saying yes might make you feel like God is asking too much from you. After the fact, saying yes may make you feel that you have lost. In Esther's case, if she walked into the king's presence without being invited, her life was over. The minute her foot crossed the threshold of his throne room, she was as good as dead unless the king extended his golden scepter.

Esther could have said, "Look, I'm the queen, now. I'm safe. It's everybody for himself."

Or she could have said, "Hey, I'm spiritual. I don't get involved in political problems."

Or she could have piously told Mordecai, "All we have to do is pray. I'm not going to risk my life when prayer is the key to our salvation. Just get everyone praying, and you won't need my help."

Mordecai probably smiled when she started making excuses. "Esther, it's like this. If you don't go and represent us, God will give us an answer from someone else, but you're going to lose your life for being quiet."

Thank the Lord, Esther wrote back and said, "OK, I'll go, and if I perish, I perish."

What is God asking you to do? Why don't you consider saying yes to whatever He has given you to do at this time? Why don't you say yes to His still, small voice? Saying yes does not mean you won't be affected by the circumstances; more likely it means you will be. Esther knew very well what the effect of her actions could be, but her fear was overcome by her strong faith in the all-knowing, all-righteous God.

Let me remind you of something very important. Do you know who we are in this world? One amusing cartoon I've saved shows a pompous lawyer reading a client's last will and testament to a group of greedy relatives. The caption reads, "I, John Jones, being of sound mind and body, spent it all."

When Jesus Christ wrote His last will and testament for His church, He made it possible for us to share His spiritual riches. Instead of spending it all, Jesus Christ paid it all. His death on the cross and His resurrection made possible the eternal salvation of our souls.

Jesus wrote us into His will; then He died so that the will would be in force. And He arose again so that He could become our heavenly advocate and so that the terms of the will would continue to be correctly followed. And do you know what God's will promises to us? We have been blessed with "every spiritual blessing in the heavenly places in Christ" (Ephesians 1:3). As Christians, we live in two dimensions, heavenly and earthly. We can't take earth to heaven with us. Instead, we have to bring heaven down here.

We receive our information from heavenly places by staying in His Word and by fellowshipping with God's people, who also have their heads in heavenly places and their feet on the earth. Ephesians 1:4 says that He has chosen us. He chose us for a purpose. We are not chance happenings. Verse 5 goes on to say that He has adopted us. All that He has became ours when we were adopted into His family.

FOR SUCH A TIME AS THIS . . .

Esther had solid, sensible reasons for not going in to see the king. According to the laws and customs of the time, it was not the thing to do. It was risky. It was asking for trouble. But God is the ruler of everything, and when He commissions us to accomplish a particular task, His timing and our obedience are the only things that matter. God was in touch with Mordecai, and Mordecai was in touch with Esther. So when Mordecai gave Esther counsel, she found the confidence and commitment she needed to accomplish the mission.

We all get weak and confused at times, and we need Mordecais in our lives. Mentoring others and receiving the mentoring of others is an essential Christian practice. Once Mordecai spoke to her, Esther came to her senses and said, "If I perish, I perish!" She placed all her confidence in the God of her people.

When Esther kept her end of the bargain, God came through,

as He always does. The king lowered his scepter. "What can I do for you?" he asked with a warm smile, offering her as much as half of his kingdom (see Esther 5:3). When we step out in faith, believing, God will pour His blessings into our lives too. But we have to believe and act on what He has called us to do. We have to have courage. We have to throw ourselves onto His mercy. *Faith that does not act is faith that is just an act.*

Once Esther really understood why she had been placed in such a high, royal position, she knew that only God could see her through. In order to move beyond that precarious place in her life, she needed more than a word from Mordecai. She needed fasting and prayer. She needed wisdom from above.

Have you been wondering when your season will finally come to an end? Sometimes our seasons do not and cannot change until we say yes to the Lord. Only then is He able to complete His work. Only then can He make the changes we've been longing to see. Only then can He move us from the Season of Growth into the Season of Harvest, where blessings, rest, and peace abound.

You see, we too have been brought into a royal position. Like Esther, we need to seek the counsel of wise Christians who love us, who are willing to mentor us. We need to seek God's will for our lives, so that He is free to steer us and guide us into our purpose. And once we know what He wants us to do, we'll need to ask our Christian friends to pray and fast for us, so we can accomplish His purpose for our lives.

Are you afraid to say yes? Don't be frightened—by trusting Him you are placing yourself in the safest possible hands. Our loving Lord will lead you to the right mate. He will give you the right job. He will look after your children. He will help you with your ministry. He will bless your efforts at church. He will make it possible for you to serve His predetermined purpose. God knows your needs before you ask. And He has a perfect plan, perfect timing, and a perfect sense of your readiness.

After months of preparation, after heeding the words of her mentor, after fasting and praying, Esther received clarity about God's purpose for her. Esther got her clear orders and direction from Him. And the words Mordecai spoke to her echo down across the centuries, reminding each of us, even today, that we have a special role to play in His kingdom. As Mordecai told Esther, we should encourage one another. After all,

> *"Who knows whether you have*
> *come to the kingdom **for such a time as this?"***
>
> —ESTHER 4:14

CHAPTER
NINE

Fulfillment

And on the second day, at the banquet of wine,
the king again said to Esther,
"What is your petition, Queen Esther?
It shall be granted you.
And what is your request, up to half my kingdom?
It shall be done!"

—ESTHER 7:2

*L*et's take a moment to review Esther's amazing story.

King Ahasuerus of Persia reigned from India to Ethiopia. Residing in this widespread dominion were large numbers of captive Israelites who had been displaced during the Babylonian captivity. At the time the story unfolded, the king of Persia was living at his winter residence at Susa, two hundred miles east of Babylon, one of several Persian capitals.

One day he asked Queen Vashti to present herself to his friends.

She refused, which brought great shame on the king and set a bad example for all the women of the kingdom. She was trying to bring in "women's liberation" for her day, and it did not work. He made the decision to divorce her. Meanwhile, God had another plan.

The Babylonians had defeated the Jews and had them in captivity for seventy years. Then Persia came along, defeated Babylon, and began ruling over the Jews. All the while, the whole kingdom was wondering who would be the next queen.

A Jewish man, Mordecai, presented his niece Esther (whom he had adopted after the death of her parents) to possibly be queen for one reason—to deliver the Jewish people out of bondage.

Haman was one of the king's closest confidants. He was plotting Mordecai's demise and the death of all the Jewish people because Mordecai would not show him the proper reverence. At about the same time, Mordecai heard of a plot to kill the king. He got word to one of the king's officers.

Esther had become quite comfortable in the palace, and her uncle had to remind her why she was there. She quickly came to see that she had no choice but to go into the king's presence and inform him about Haman's plot against her people. She prepared herself conscientiously so that she could be pleasing to the king. Taking her life in her hands, she courageously walked into the throne room. She could not be sure whether the king would lower his scepter and welcome her, or would order her immediate execution for presumptuously entering his presence without an invitation.

By God's grace, the king welcomed Esther warmly. Once she had his ear, she chose her timing and her words carefully. When she told him of Haman's plot to get rid of all the Jews, the king was enraged—especially when he discovered Haman on his knees begging Esther for forgiveness. He mistook it as an assault on the queen and ordered him killed.

Haman was hanged on the same gallows he had prepared for Mordecai. Mordecai took Haman's place in the kingdom, and in the process of all of this, God saved an entire group of people from extermination. This happened because one young Jewish girl was obedient to God's purpose and direction in her life. Esther made history because of her obedience to God. Her purpose was fulfilled when she was welcomed into the presence of the king.

KNOWING OUR FATHER, THE KING

Maybe you're saying, "Lois, you don't understand. I am anything but a queen, and I'm not aspiring to be one."

If that's your position, I beg to differ with you. Do you know Jesus Christ? Have you received Him into your heart and asked Him to forgive your sins? If so, you are a daughter of the Most High God, the King of Creation. You have been adopted into His royal family. He has invited you into His presence so that you can know Him better and love Him more.

That raises another important question: How well do you know the Lord? Have you spent enough time in His presence and in His Word to really appreciate Him for who He is? Let's take a look at what the Bible says about Him. What is our heavenly Father—the King of Kings and Lord of Lords—really like?

First of all, *He is sovereign.* Psalm 93:1 says, "The Lord reigns, He is clothed with majesty; the Lord is clothed, He has girded Himself with strength. Surely the world is established, so that it cannot be moved."

Second, the Bible speaks of *God's providence.* Sometimes we call providence "the invisible hand of the Lord." Even when we can't see Him, we find evidence of His work in our lives and in the world. "We know that all things work together for good to those who love God, to those who are the called according to His purpose" (Romans 8:28). God is actively at work in all the circumstances of our lives, both good and bad, whether we know it or not.

There is a conspicuous absence of God's name throughout the book of Esther. Yet as we reflect upon the story line, it is clear that God is the One responsible for all the good, all the justice, all the victory that takes place. Whenever God seems far away, we can turn to some important instructions in James 4:8: "Draw near to God and He will draw near to you." Psalm 145:18 affirms, "The Lord is near to all who call upon Him, to all who call upon Him in truth."

Third, we discover that *God has foreknowledge.* Ephesians 1:4–5 explains, "He chose us in Him before the foundation of the world, that we should be holy and without blame before Him in love." Our Lord sees the future before it takes place. He decides what the future will be. Isn't that a God to serve? You can get up every morning and anticipate His new mercies and know that He has your future under control.

Fourth, we find that our *God is just.* "For we know Him who said, 'Vengeance is Mine, I will repay,' says the Lord. And again, 'The Lord will judge His people'" (Hebrews 10:30). Our God is a God of justice.

Fifth, as we read His Word and spend time in His presence, we find that *God is omnipotent*. That means that He is all-powerful. "Jesus looked at them and said to them, 'With men this is impossible, but with God all things are possible'" (Matthew 19:26). God can do anything and everything that does not contradict His nature.

Sixth, our *God is omnipresent*. The Lord is everywhere. He is everywhere we are, and everywhere we are not; we can never leave His presence. "If I ascend into heaven, You are there; if I make my bed in hell, behold, You are there" (Psalm 139:8). God inhabits the whole universe. There is no place where He is not.

Seventh, *God is omniscient*. He knows everything there is to know. "He counts the number of the stars; He calls them all by name. Great is our Lord, and mighty in power; His understanding is infinite" (Psalm 147:4–5). God knows everything actual and potential, past, present, and future. Wow! Aren't you happy that you have such a King, who has called you to the kingdom . . . for such a time as this?

Our God, for All Seasons

What time is it in your life? Are you busily planting new seeds? Are you enduring (or enjoying) a prolonged period of preparation? Are you restlessly waiting for new life to burst up through the soil, gradually growing into healthy, strong plants?

Living in our seasons requires us to learn lessons in patience. Sometimes we think of patience as a virtue we need in dealing with difficult people or circumstances. And that's true. We have to be patient with other people's unruly kids, with older folks who drone on and on about their surgeries, and with our own aches and pains and worries and woes.

The Bible also tells us that we need to wait with patience *on the Lord* (Psalm 37:7). As our seasons pass, and we grow weary of the responsibilities and requirements they entail, we become anxious to move on. We feel that we have taken good care of the soil. We have done a painstaking job of planting and watering. We have allowed Him to work on us—inside and out—in preparation for the future. We can't see any reason to remain in our present season, except for one small detail: He hasn't yet told us to move into the next one. At this point, the word *patience* begins to take on a whole new meaning.

The poet who wrote Psalm 27 seems to have experienced the need to wait on God. He describes his weariness, his readiness to give up. He wrote, "I would have lost heart, unless I had believed that I would see the goodness of the Lord in the land of the living. Wait on the Lord; be of good courage, and He shall strengthen your heart; wait, I say, on the Lord!" (vv. 13–14).

What are some of the circumstances in your life that are making you feel uncomfortable? Inside what palace are you locked up? Have you explored every nook and cranny of your living space? Have you appreciated the beauties of the furnishings and accessories the King has provided for you?

What season are you in? Besides the seasons of planting, growth, and harvest, we also have four seasons in each year: spring, summer, fall, and winter. It bears repeating—we can sit in the Texas sun on a hot summer day and complain about how uncomfortable it is. Or we can dress in cool clothes, move into the shade, and enjoy a glass of cool lemonade. There's a purpose for each season of our lives, and many blessings that accompany that purpose. And there's no point in trying to experience June in January.

How does God operate in our seasons? Maybe this acrostic will help us remember God's intentions for us as we allow Him to work in our lives—according to His calendar.

SOVEREIGNTY OF GOD.

God controlled the circumstances of Esther's life, even though His name does not appear in the book of Esther.

We don't always see God at work in our lives, either. But He is sovereign and rules over all things. Nothing comes into our lives without His approval. And nothing bad happens in our lives that He does not transform into good (Romans 8:28). God is the great Designer of heaven and earth, of your life and of mine. He is the master Artist who makes all things beautiful in His time (Ecclesiastes 3:11). He is the Composer of the song "the morning stars sang together" (Job 38:7), the One who puts a new song of praise in our hearts after He rescues us and plants our feet on solid ground (Psalm 40:2–3).

E LEVATION BY GOD.

Esther found favor in King Ahasuerus's sight because God made her beautiful, provided her with the proper preparation, and placed her in a strategic position.

God's Word is full of stories about His preference for lifting up humble people into unexpectedly powerful and influential roles. Jesus' mother Mary spoke of this when she praised God for His miraculous gift to her, choosing her to be the mother of His only begotten Son:

"My soul magnifies the Lord,
And my spirit has rejoiced
in God my Savior.
For He has regarded the lowly state
of His maidservant;
For behold, henceforth all generations will call me blessed.
For He who is mighty has done
great things for me,
And holy is His name.
And His mercy is on
those who fear Him
From generation to generation.
He has shown strength with His arm;
He has scattered the proud in the imagination of their hearts.
He has put down the mighty
from their thrones,
And exalted the lowly.
He has filled the hungry with good things,
And the rich He has sent away empty."

—LUKE 1:46–53

When we humble ourselves before the Lord, when we admit that without Him we can do nothing (John 15:5), He begins to act. His strength is made perfect in our weakness (2 Corinthians 12:9). He takes us by the hand, lifts us up, and brings us into places we could never have reached on our own. That way, we have no choice but to say, "It had to be God!"

A SSISTANCE FROM GOD.
God gave Mordecai to Esther for wisdom and encouragement.

God will also provide us with help and encouragement from among His people if we will receive it, hear it, listen to it, and obey Him through it. We live in a culture that applauds independence and self-reliance, and we sometimes feel insulted by the idea that we need help from others. "I'd rather do it myself!" an old advertising slogan declares. And we laugh in approval.

The fact is, God never intended for His people to function in isolation. The description of the body of Christ we find in 1 Corinthians 12 makes it very clear that we really do need each other. We are to make decisions with the help of many advisors (Proverbs 15:22); we are to confess our faults to one another (James 5:16); and younger women are to learn from older women (Titus 2:3–5). Mentoring is a biblical principle. And if you'll ask Him, God will provide a mentor for you.

S UBMISSION TO GOD.
Esther fasted and prayed when she heard about the deadly edict that had been published against her people.

Praying and fasting is more than a ritual or a way of getting God's attention. It serves the purpose of submitting our bodies—which are weakened by the lack of food—to God, who is our strength. When we choose to forego food for spiritual reasons, we are submitting to His power and renouncing our own.

Prayer and fasting also does a mysterious work in the spiritual realm where, the Bible tells us, our struggle really is centered. "We do not wrestle against flesh and blood, but against principalities, against powers, against the rulers of the darkness of this age, against spiritual hosts of wickedness in the heavenly places" (Ephesians

6:12). On one occasion, when the disciples were unable to cast out a demon, Jesus told them, "This kind does not go out except by prayer and fasting" (Matthew 17:15–21). Even today when we are faced with difficult spiritual challenges, we would be wise to heed His words.

OPPORTUNITIES FROM GOD.

God could have defeated Haman and destroyed his plot against the Jews through supernatural means. Instead, He gave Mordecai and Esther the opportunity and privilege of being a part of His work of salvation.

God has graciously included us, His children, in His plans for the salvation of the world. He wants to bless us by allowing us to share His joyful work of bringing others to know Him, of teaching and discipling them, and of instructing them in how to live according to His Word.

Are we using the opportunities God gives us? Esther could have overlooked her opportunity by being either too comfortable or too scared. Don't those same issues get in the way of our opportunities to serve God? Nothing is more important than being part of His great and mighty work of salvation. Let's not miss the blessing that accompanies every opportunity He gives us.

NEEDS MET BY GOD.

God took care of Esther's needs, even though she couldn't see what He was doing at the time.

God allowed Vashti to be removed as queen, so Esther could be in the right place at the right time (Esther 1). Esther had no control over Vashti's rather surprising decision to take a sudden stand for women's liberation. She certainly couldn't have plotted Vashti's demise. In fact, at the time it probably had never occurred to Esther that *she* could become the queen of Persia. That was beyond her wildest dreams.

God caused the king to wake up in the night, and in the king's wakefulness, God reminded him of Mordecai's faithfulness (Esther 6:1–3). Esther could not have done anything about Mordecai's reputation, especially in the middle of the night when she was in the palace of the women. But God knew very well what lay ahead, and He caused King Ahasuerus to suffer from insomnia. That prepared the way for Mordecai to be honored, and for Haman to be discredited.

God allowed Haman to build the gallows that would be used for his own execution. Sometimes, from our perspective, we think God is letting things go too far. We wonder why He doesn't step in sooner and put a stop to some of the world's injustices. But God can see the end from the beginning (Isaiah 46:10), and at times He uses the weapons of the wicked for His own purposes, causing evil people to be slain with their own swords (Psalm 37:15).

The more we trust God to meet our needs, the less likely we are to try to meet them ourselves, with disastrous results. He has promised to supply all our needs through Jesus (Philippians 4:19). Do we believe His promise or don't we?

S ALVATION BY GOD.
 The Jews were delivered because of God's faithfulness, Mordecai's wisdom, and Esther's courageous obedience.

When we allow God to work in our lives according to His plans, according to the seasons of His choosing, we find that salvation has come to our house. Salvation isn't just a matter of receiving eternal life, although that's certainly its ultimate purpose.

Salvation rescues us from the earthly traps that sometimes snare us (Psalm 18:4–18).

Salvation delivers us from our enemies (Psalm 59:1).

Salvation helps us overcome our old sin nature (Romans 7–8).

Salvation protects us from many of the dangers that surround us (Psalm 91).

Salvation keeps us from being made ashamed (Isaiah 54:4).

Salvation provides opportunity for healing and good health (Psalm 103:2–3).

Salvation allows us to become more like Jesus, transforming us into His image (1 John 3:2).

Salvation makes it possible for us to receive God's best for us, both in this life and in the life to come. As the seasons come and go, we learn more and more what it means to trust Him. We discover what it means to see His hand on our lives. Like Esther, the captive who became queen, we experience what it means to know the One "who is able," as Paul wrote,

> *to do exceedingly abundantly above all that we ask or think,*
> *according to the power that works in us,*
> *to Him be glory in the church by Christ Jesus*
> *throughout all ages, world without end. Amen.*
> —EPHESIANS 3:20–21

CONTACT AMBASSADOR ENTERPRISES

P.O. Box 763160
Dallas, TX 75376-3160

AmbassEnt@aol.com
1 (888) 467-7415

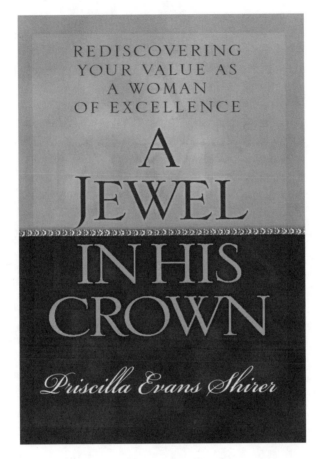

A Jewel in His Crown

Rediscovering Your Value as a Woman of Excellence

When they become weary and discouraged, women lose sight of their real value as beloved daughters of God. *A Jewel in His Crown* examines how the way women view their worth deeply affects their relationships. This book teaches women how to renew strength and be women of excellence.

Quality Paperback 0-8024-4097-5

Moody Press, a ministry of Moody Bible Institute,
is designed for education, evangelization, and edification.
If we may assist you in knowing more about Christ
and the Christian life, please write us without obligation:
Moody Press, c/o MLM, Chicago, Illinois 60610.